The Diary of a Hapless Father:

Graham Peterson

Pete Sortwell

ISBN-13:978-1493715411
ISBN-10:1493715410

DEDICATION

For my mate, Pete ~~Smith~~. Will Watt :)

Pete Sortwell

ACKNOWLEDGEMENTS

I wouldn't be able to get my work into your hands if it wasn't for the help of the team I employ, they work extremely hard to make sure what ends up on your kindle is a high quality. These people are:

Julie Lewthwaite, for her continued sterling work on turning my ramblings into something that I can charge money for.

http://www.mlwritingservices.co.uk/

Graham D. Lock, for the excellent covers he's provided me.

http://www.peopleperhour.com/people/graham-d/animator-graphic-designer-and-illu/177926

Finally, thanks to Jack Dean for his input on this when I was stuck. If you fancy a laugh, check out his YouTube Channel http://www.youtube.com/user/JaackMaate

I can't recommend each and every one of these people enough.

INTRODUCTION

This is my second diary. I've misplaced the first. I think Keith, my so called best friend, has stolen it. He's always struck me as a literature thief.

Just in case I don't find it again: I started the last diary as I was about to become a father. The mother of my baby, Alison, and I had only been together for a matter of weeks before she fell pregnant. It wasn't a recipe for success, but it seems to have worked thus far.

SEPTEMBER 2012

Tuesday September 25th 2012

5.00 a.m.

I've just got home from the hospital. Charlie Peterson is now with us. He's great. Tiny little ears, tiny little hands and big brown eyes looking up at the world. I read in my book that I bought to help me cope with the pregnancy that he can't actually see anything at the moment, but I'm not so sure, his eyes seem pretty focused to me. A little glazed, if anything, like a doughnut. He's got a full head of hair, too, more than me, even. I was holding him less than an hour ago. Alison and Charlie have headed down to the mother and baby ward now. I was told to go home and get some sleep as I'd started staggering about an hour after he was born. Mother and baby are OK, though, that's the main thing. The birth was awful, but I can't bring myself to talk about that now.

9.30 a.m.

So, the birth:

We arrived at the hospital about ten to nine yesterday morning. I'd not slept more than five minutes at a stretch as I was worried about what was happening next to me, although Alison seemed to sleep with no problems at all, only waking up once to move about a bit and go to the lav. In films the contractions seem to be a lot more violent than they were in reality; I still wasn't sure she was having them. But we were at the hospital, so everything was going to be OK.

Or so I thought. Once the obligatory three hours' wait had passed, the midwife on duty took one look at Alison (down there) and told us we needed to go home again until she was seven centimetres dilated. I was already pissed off before we even heard that, but the stony faced cow's standard 'don't care, I've said all I'm saying' response to every attempt I made to get her to change her mind really wound me up. She was sending us home and that was that. I was fully prepared to collapse and then let them deal with me, but Alison suggested it might not be helpful to do that, so I loaded her back into the car and aimed it towards home.

We didn't even make it out of the car park before Alison was screaming like there was a knife attacker in the back of the car with her. The calm lady that had suggested it best I not throw myself to the floor barely five minutes earlier had suddenly turned into devil woman. The screaming and name calling was definitely post-watershed stuff; I was told I needed to 'get the fucking car back in the pissing car park now', which was more difficult to do than you'd think: I was on a single carriageway road. Looking back, I can see it was a bad idea to try and do a three-point turn. I'm not that good at them at the best of times, but in those noisy conditions I ended up forgetting to turn the wheel before I moved the car again. I wasn't counting, but it was more like a thirty-seven-point turn by the time I finished. I also lost the indicator from the front nearside. By the time I got back to the hospital car park I didn't even bother paying for a ticket, or in fact finding a proper parking bay. I just wanted to get out of the enclosed space where all the screaming was going on. I suppose it was good practise for what was to come, although I suspect Charlie will have less violent intent behind his racket.

Nurse Miserable was at the door of the ward when we got back there; I'm not sure if it was the look on my face or the way Alison walked, but she didn't say anything like she'd been reeling off before. I think she must have realised she'd been stupid to send us away in the first place. I was mentally noting it all down. Heads were going to roll when I got out of there and managed to write a strongly worded letter.

They took us straight through to the ward, got Alison on the bed and went off to do something. It was the last we saw of them for two hours. Alison was going in and out of screaming fits, as were the other women on the ward. I went off a few times looking for a nurse, doctor, midwife, or indeed anyone that looked like they worked there. On the occasions that I found someone, they explained that it was extremely busy and that they'd be along as soon as they could. Every time I had to go back to Alison and tell her that I couldn't get her any pain relief and I couldn't help her, it was awful. I did think about going into the street and seeing if I could score some heroin. I've heard that's a good pain killer. Alison told me to shut up when I asked her 'where the fuck is everyone?' loud enough for the whole ward to hear. The next time I went looking for someone I saw several blokes in the same position as me, all looking up the corridor waiting for someone to come and help their partners.

I imagine the camps Hitler killed all the Jews in had a similar atmosphere to that ward. People just looking for help that never came, it was horrible feeling powerless to help. Things seemed to have slowed down for us over the past hour spent waiting. I don't know why, maybe that's what happens. Hollywood has a lot to answer for. They'd tricked me into thinking: get to the hospital, scream, push, baby – done. It isn't like that, though. Lord knows, it isn't.

There must have been a shift change, because all of a sudden we had staff all over the ward, all attending to the women. I could hear them tell the woman across from us to stop pushing as she wasn't in the labour room; she was wheeled away sharpish and within a couple of minutes they announced that she'd given birth.

It was our turn next. *It was happening.* Alison was taken into the delivery room and I followed shortly after; first I had to run and get a pasty from the machine at the other end of the six mile corridor. By the time I got back things were well underway. Legs were up, and Alison was sucking on the gas and air tube like her life depended on it. I asked if they were going to get the real drugs out once the contractions started, only to be stared at by the nurse.

'It's Alison's choice,' she told me, before making herself busy. I looked at Alison, who had her eyes scrunched shut and looked like she was in a lot of pain. I pointed to the green papers and asked the nurse to check the back page, where it clearly stated that I knew the birthing plan and would be asking for the pain relief. I'm still not sure how exactly it happened, but within a couple of seconds I was having a stand up row with the midwife.

If I had a button to push to win arguments I'd use it all the time. I don't, though, and the midwife did; she called in the cavalry and before I knew it there were three more midwives, and a couple of porters who looked like they smoked more than half the people in the mortuary did.

All I was asking for was the epidural that was on the birth plan and they threatened to remove me. I won in the end, as the head midwife told me the anaesthetist was on the way.

That wasn't a lie, but when she got there she informed us that she was only popping in for a chat before heading to A&E, where it was really busy. I asked what good she thought a chat would do my partner, who by this point had started crying. She just shrugged and went off, promising she'd be back.

The relationship between me and the midwife in the room never really improved; by the time the doctor started showing up, I'd been standing over a helpless Alison for about fifteen hours. The only thing of use I could do was give her sips of water when the contractions stopped. Things changed in the room when the doctor was there; people started milling about. The doctor knew what she was doing, she knew how to speak to me, and she gave very clear, direct and confident instructions to her team.

At that moment, at 4 a.m., I knew I was going to be getting a look at my son within the next hour. I started to feel a bit overwhelmed and the doctor asked if I was OK. I held my eyes as wide as they would go to make sure the tears didn't fall and maintained my male stance.

It was happening; mind you, the pushing had been happening for a while, although in the times that Alison could find the strength to talk, she complained about being too tired to push. The doctor seemed to breathe new life into us all. She told Alison what she needed her to do and she told her the time that it was going to take, which was something none of the other medical professionals had been prepared to do. A trolley was brought in containing all the things you'd expect to see on a trolley being wheeled into a birthing room, and some that I'd never seen before. It was just then that the doctor didn't *announce* that she could see the head, like I've seen on the TV, she asked if 'Dad' wanted to have a look at the head. I couldn't say 'no', but I wanted to. I'd managed to keep at the top end until then. I did have a glance, though, as I didn't want to disobey the doctor. If I'm honest, I couldn't really make out a head, it was a bit of a mess down there, and I am struggling to think about it now as I write.

Needless to say, as soon as I could I went back up to the top end and held the gas and air pipe for Alison. It was at such an angle, and the pipe was made of such tough tubing, that it was always wanting to bend the other way. I was getting cramp, but I couldn't not give her it. I was glad when Alison started screaming at me to 'get that useless fucking pipe' out of her face. It wasn't long after that, that the doctor got excited and told us that after three more pushes she was going to pull the baby out. The head was out at that point. I couldn't hear screaming, but I didn't have time to be worried because the doctor told us it was time; she grabbed a knife, cut something or other and then yanked my son out with a pair of forceps.

Then I heard the screaming. A little, white, soggy baby appeared and was handed straight to Alison, who looked in wonder at the child that was now in her arms. If I forget everything else in my life, the look on Alison's face when she first met our son is the one thing that I'd want to keep hold of. It was amazing. The first thing I noticed about the baby was his head. It was a funny shape. The shape of a cycle helmet. I was later assured that it was only like that for the birth and would go back to normal after a couple of days.

And I didn't faint, like Boris had suggested I probably would. He only said that because I did faint one time when I walked into the staff toilets after he'd been in there having one of his gentleman's sit downs.

I got shoved in the corner while everyone had a look at the baby, checked it over and cleaned up the poo he did pretty much instantly. It was then I thought I'd have a seat; I'd been on my feet for ages and they hurt. I sat down and stared at the floor, reflecting on everything that had just happened. It was an experience I'd never had before and at that moment in time I swore to myself I wouldn't do it again. I looked up and saw the doctor remove the afterbirth; it was then that I was sick in my mouth a bit. It was like the really awful part in the film, *Alien*. The doctor calling it 'breakfast' didn't help. And I had to swallow the sick.

Shortly after I was sick, Alison was also sick. I hadn't realised, but I'd fed her about three litres of water over the last few hours. The sick went on the baby a bit and that's when it was decided that I could have a hold of my son, which I did. He was so delicate. So small and so, so angry. I've never thought about what it must be like to be born, but I should think it's an absolutely terrifying experience. All of a sudden you're forced out of somewhere nice, warm and dark, with food on tap and no need to ever go to the toilet, into a bright room where someone in rubber gloves is just waiting for the chance to slap the shit out of you … literally. I bet it's freezing, too, like when you step out of a shower. He stopped crying for a while when I was holding him and went back to sleep. Then a nurse grabbed his feet and jammed a needle right into his heel which made him squeal for a minute before he went quiet. I wondered what they'd given him, thinking it must be some heavy duty shit for him to pass out straight away. We were assured he was OK and that it was just some harmless vitamin K that all babies are given. She then took him off me and got him dressed. I was able to see Alison; she'd finished having her downstairs sorted out and was padded up. She looked shattered. Shattered, but content. We were a family and without saying it, we knew we were linked together forever.

I got my phone out and took a couple of pictures, which I sent out to the people that had asked for them, then I asked if it was OK if I went home, as I was really tired and to be honest I wanted to get out of the way of the midwives. I knew that Alison would be moved to the mother and baby unit soon and up there they'd have different staff. I started to feel a little bit guilty about the outbursts I'd made throughout the night due to the utter incompetence of the hospital staff, but deep down I knew that we'd been given a substandard service and I didn't want to find myself apologising for questioning it. Alison was fine with it and was going to start to see if she could start feeding Charlie when I left. There was someone there to help her do it and her motherly instinct had kicked in. I gave them both a kiss and headed outside to ring our parents and let them know the news. I rang my folks first and discovered that all four parents were together and waiting for the call before they opened some champagne. It was a bit weird, but I didn't really think too much about it. I just tried to remember where it was I'd left my car.

So that's how it happened. I'm now just about to leave the house and go and see my son again. I'd promised myself I'd get a decent sleep, but to be honest, I couldn't get to sleep as I was thinking about my son. I was thinking about all the things we're going to get up to in the years to come. All my hopes and dreams for him and us as a family. I was thinking about the family holidays I'd had as a child and how I hoped I'd be a good enough father to be able to recreate that for Charlie.

When I did wake up I had a message from Alison. It was a picture of Charlie and the message said, *'We love you, Daddy. Sleep tight. Visiting is at 10 a.m. Can you bring babygros? x'*

I'd only been out for a couple of hours, but my brain wasn't interested in letting me go back to sleep, so I hauled myself up and made a coffee before sitting down and waiting for 10 a.m. I was going to sit down and write a long complaint letter, but I've decided that I'm not really interested in getting the inevitable reply that tells me they don't really care and that they haven't the money to make it better. It would just be a massive waste of time.

I'm going to see my son now.

10.30 p.m.

I went looking for babygros before I headed to the hospital. I bypassed Tesco as I thought it would be too busy and hold me up from seeing my son. I shouldn't have been so hasty. The

Boots nearest to the hospital must know people are always looking for new babygros after not being able to find the ones they were supposed to have at home: they sold packs of three and only in yellow. I had a decision to make there and then, get them or turn up empty handed. I also didn't have the teddy I'd been thinking about buying for the last few weeks. I got the babygros and headed to the till. I didn't know whether to laugh or cry when the numbers came up at £18.99. I could have sworn the shelf said they were a fiver. Still, I didn't have time to argue as I'd decided that I needed to get a teddy. If I didn't, then what sort of father would I be? I thought about the teddy Keith had given me for the baby; maybe I could use that and just tell Charlie that I'd bought it. It would be dishonest, though, and I don't think any kind of relationship can be run that way. Keith told me once that he knew someone who pretended to be blind to get a girlfriend. I doubt that worked out well; how could it?

I ended up driving all the way back to Tesco and getting some cheaper and bluer babygros, then I had to go all the way into town to get the teddy as Tesco seem to sell everything but teddies these days. I ended up choosing a little furry thing that had its name stapled to its foot. His name is Brian and there are no parts on him that can be pulled off and eaten, apparently. Well, except for the leaflet that gave me that information.

Charlie was struggling to feed when I got there. Alison was worried so I pressed the alarm near the bed and all the babies in the ward started crying. I think they could probably do with a quieter alarm in that ward, if I'm honest, as throughout the day I needed to call them a few times and every time it upset all the little ones. Not Charlie, as he was already upset. When he wasn't upset he was either eating, being forced to eat, sleeping, or crying. He didn't really do much else. I didn't feel comfortable in the ward, it felt like they were keeping him there so they could keep an eye on us and make sure we weren't going to end up on the news for doing something terrible. Once I picked him up to give Alison a break and one of the nurses was walking past; Charlie started screaming the place down as soon as I touched him. It felt like I must have been hurting him. I hope he doesn't hate me already.

At three it was time for the regular visitors. At one minute past we had both sets of grandparents by the bed, I asked them if they'd been waiting by the ward door for three o'clock to strike and they confirmed that they'd actually been in the hospital since midday. They'd eaten here and then my father had taken Alison's dad to look at the oldest part of the building as he was convinced there were gargoyles on the roof, while the grandmas had opted for having an in-depth conversation with the Women's Institute about jam making and how they could go about joining up. I didn't get to hear if any gargoyles had been found as one of the midwives turned up and told us that only two visitors were allowed at a time. We did try and protest, but it was clear from the look on the midwife's face that it wasn't going to work. I took the granddads for a coffee. It was while we were walking up to the café that I noticed the two must have been having a 'let's see who can bring the biggest camera to the hospital' competition. They both had absolutely huge, paparazzi-style cameras. I didn't even bother trying to ask them what they thought they'd be doing with the pictures. I'm sure one or both of them had delusions of selling them to the local paper as images of the most beautiful baby ever born. Seriously, they'd only seen Charlie for a few seconds, but they were more excited than I was. They were comparing noses with each other and arguing over which side of the family the eyes, ears and mouth came from. Once we'd sat down with a coffee it all went quiet as they perused the shots they'd managed to take before we were thrown out the ward. Bill said he could even edit the photo on his camera without the need for PhotoShop.

'I thought about that one myself, but the lack of megapixels put me off in the end,' my father told him.

'Get yours second hand off eBay, did you?' Bill asked, looking at the chipped corner of his counterpart's gadget.

'No, I dropped it when you shut the door on me as we got out the car,' my father reminded him.

God, they'd actually been racing to be the first to get to the ward. I suppose I should be glad that there are two sets of grandparents that are eager to see the latest member of their family.

'So when you get married, he'll officially be a Peterson,' my dad said after they'd finished squabbling.

'A Peterson, with the name of a Tilly. Charles has long been a name of choice in the Tilly family,' Bill said, not wanting to be outdone. I think we all knew he was clutching at straws, though, Dad had played the royal flush and there was nothing he could do about it. Charlie would have my name. I know that, as I'm the one that's going to the registry office.

The grandmothers joined us after about half an hour and said that we needed to wait a while before going back in, as Alison was trying to give Charlie a feed another way, The midwife was showing her how to hold him like a rugby ball or something. The women brought with them a calming influence. Both the grandfathers showed off the pictures they'd taken on the little screens on the backs of their cameras and the grandmothers were the exact opposite of how their partners had been. 'I think he has Alison's eyes,' my mother said, while Alison's mother, Sue, said that she thought he had my nose.

Once the grandmothers had let us know sufficient time had elapsed that we could go back to the ward, I took them down. The midwife didn't mind me being there as I wasn't a normal visitor, I was the father. I turned to give my father the look that meant for the first time I was more important than him and we both got the giggles. Bob saw this as a perfect opportunity to look like a tit and got down on one knee and started clicking away. I'm looking forward to getting the photo printed; it'll be nice to put in Charlie's room.

The granddads were different in the ward where Alison was. Of course, her own father wasn't thinking about being better, he was in father mode himself. It was nice to be able to understand that on a new level. I could see a tear in his eye as he was hugging his daughter, who was holding Charlie.

Once it was my father's turn to hold him and say hello, Charlie did the biggest fart I've ever heard from a child. Again this made us all laugh, although the laughing didn't last long as it became quite apparent from my father's face that we needed to change Charlie. The grandparents pulled the 'we'd better be off' card and left me to deal with the tiny but deadly poo Charlie had produced. It seemed to relax him, though, and he stretched his little arms out, going back to sleep before I'd even finished changing his nappy. I thought it would be difficult to clean him up and put a new nappy on, but it's not as hard as it looks. I was proud of myself until Alison complained of feeling warm water on her about an hour later. I didn't know there were two sticky labels on both sides. They should be clearly marked. When she came to help change all the sheets, the midwife said it happens to lots of dads. I noticed she said 'dads' and not 'mums'.

They're keeping Charlie and Alison in as he is a little yellow. I worried as that's what George Best used to look like, but apparently it's normal. In Jamaica they pop the babies outside for half hour to soak up the sun's rays and get some vitamin D. We don't have any kinds of vitamins coming out the sky in England, though, so they had to put him in a little bed with lights underneath. He slept happily in there until it was time to force one of Alison's nipples in his mouth again.

I wasn't sure if I should stay, but Alison said I needed to leave as it was time for all the mothers to talk about how the fathers were. I'm not sure if she was messing about or not. I imagined the nurses wheeling them all together in some spare ward or other and them all sitting about like an AA meeting slagging us off. There'd be one, of course, that didn't have any problems at all and whose man was perfect throughout. Then it would get worse for all the other men and the new mothers would spend the rest of the meeting planning out how they were going to get us back. I'm sure they don't really do things like that, but Alison did want to be left alone with the midwife so she could teach her about breastfeeding and the best way to hold a baby.

When I left I could feel all the new mothers' eyes following me. It's not my fault that the midwives took so long to come that I pressed the alarm three or four times. I didn't give any eye contact to them, but I did hear someone call me a wanker.

All in all the day was OK. The hospital food I had for dinner was fairly dreadful. It reminded me of school dinners – on a bad day. It was like they'd employed Boris, the drunken Russian who works in the same kitchen I do, and he was doing all the cooking. I went for sausages, beans and chips. That was my mistake, thinking that they couldn't get something so basic wrong. The beans looked they'd been cooking longer than Charlie had been in Alison's belly. The sausages had been under the heat light too long, and the chips had been cooked in a fryer that seemed to be cleaned less often than the one at work. I ate it anyway.

I promised Alison that I wouldn't be going out to wet the baby's head with her dad. He'd threatened to show up at the hospital and take me out when Alison spoke to him this morning; he never showed up, though. I think he was probably too busy wetting his own head with whatever he could get his hands on. I just came home and had a lager shandy on my own. I'm going to have an early night tonight.

11.30 p.m.

I can't sleep. I keep thinking about Charlie's little face. I'm going to try hot milk, hopefully that'll get me off.

11.45 p.m.

A text from Alison asking why I'd bought double the amount of babygros, and why were some yellow. I replied to say I got all I could and told her not to worry about it. She texted back a smiley face, so she is OK.

Wednesday September 26th 2012

I got a few hours' sleep on and off last night. I kept waking up thinking I'd slept in, only to realise that I'd only been asleep for a few minutes. It was all fairly depressing, although not as bad as, say, a really hot summer where you toss and turn all night, only to wake up sweating and thinking you're in a coffin ten minutes after finally dropping off. However depressing and fearful I was when I woke up, though, it was lifted immensely by the thought that I now have a son.

I headed into the hospital via McDonald's. Alison said they'd given her toast for breakfast that was as soft as fresh bread. Honestly, how can you mess up toast? It's probably the easiest thing there is to heat up. I know people burn it, but I've never known it go floppy before. I got myself a couple of double espressos while I was getting the breakfast muffins. The first was so hot my tongue was still hurting this evening. It was only when I pulled away and saw brown liquid running down the back window that I remembered I'd put the second one on the roof of the car to cool down while I ate my breakfast. Alison's car doesn't have a rear window wiper and I have nothing to clean it up with, so I just left nature and wind power to do their jobs and take it off. It didn't, though. It just stained it, then dried the stain.

Alison called me selfish for not waiting to eat my muffin with her (cold). I didn't take it on board, though, I've read that new mothers have hormones all over the place and if I was in hospital, I wouldn't mind her shoving two sausage and egg muffins into her mouth before bringing me mine. Charlie was just lying about in his little sunbed most of the day. I've read that babies can't see much in the first few days, but I'm fairly sure he was looking at me today; even when I wasn't saying anything, he was looking at my face.

I still can't get over the fact I now have a son. He's just a lovely boy, too. I didn't think it was possible to love something as much as I love him. I've played out scenarios in my head about people trying to harm him. I was thinking today about that nurse who killed kids and was arrested for it in the 80s. I found myself daydreaming about what would happen if one of the ones in the hospital did that. I found myself living out the situation mentally and pushing a few people down the stairs, screaming at doctors and blaming them. The daydream only stopped when Alison asked me why I was giving death stares to her favourite midwife.

This afternoon I headed into town to register little Charlie's birth. There was little else going on at the hospital. The only reason Alison is worried now is that he isn't feeding so well and I seem to just get in the way when the midwives are helping. The jaundice has subsided a lot and he's now almost a normal colour all the time.

Before I went to the council offices, I needed to go home and get all the documents that I'd forgotten to pick up on the way in. Once I'd done that all I had to do was check into the 'one stop shop' which I think is code for 'we can't be arsed to hire specialists' and wait for an hour and a half while all the housing benefit claimants got their rent payments sorted out.

When I did finally get into the room, the registrar was lovely. She talked to me about what her job was and why liked doing it, then, when she was writing out the birth certificate, she showed me the old style way in which they still sign their name. She used blotting paper, which is a bit like kitchen roll, to make sure the ink from the fountain pen she was using didn't smudge. Everything else on the certificate was printed from a computer. Not like mine, which is handwritten all the way through.

I opted for both the full and short versions and handed over my thirty pieces of silver (£8). The registrar said that we could make changes to the certificate for £3 in the first eighteen months of Charlie's life, if we were to Christen him or add a middle name.

Until I was sitting in front of the registrar I hadn't even thought about middle names or what sort of religion, if any, we were going to bring Charlie up to be. There are so many to choose from. It's a fairly easy process to narrow it down, though; I mean, we're both English and were both brought up Church of England, so none of the more cosmopolitan or plain weird religions are ever going to be anything to worry about. The choice really comes down to this: do we instil in our child a sense of being a Christian and tell him that there is a God in the world, or do we get real about it and not bother? I remember being a child and taking great comfort from knowing, or thinking, that there was something more powerful out there creating things and making the world turn round. But then, over time, as bad things happened and not everyone was as nice as me, it was a disappointment.

Walking back from the hospital I was thinking about my faith. I think I have more of a '999' view on religion and God; if I need it and I'm in trouble, then I will ask for help. I've no idea if it works though, there are so many variants. I then thought about how selfish of me it was to think like this, as I suppose anything that lowers a child's natural anxiety about the world they're getting to know is a good thing. If Charlie is able to have a more relaxed time through believing in God, then he should do that. Then, when he's old enough, he will make his own mind up about that sort of thing. I popped into a bookshop and read one of the titles on religion. I think I'm what's known as an agnostic. I don't firmly believe there isn't any way whatsoever there's a God, I'm kind of indifferent and waiting for a sign or something. I suppose the gift of a new life is sign enough for some people, but maybe I've watched too much David Attenborough over the years, as new life is just nature, it's how it works. Things reproduce, it just happens.

I'm going to speak to Alison about it when we're all home and settled. Maybe I should go and see a vicar and see if they can make any sense of it.

When I got back to the ward, Alison and Charlie were both asleep. Marge, the woman in the next bed, was awake, though, and eating a lovely smelling curry that someone had brought in for her. She offered me a plate. I normally would have felt bad taking food off someone in hospital, but it did smell good and there was a huge Tupperware container full, so I had some.

As Alison slept on, Marge told me about where she grew up. She's from South Africa originally and came over when she went to university in London. I asked where her partner was and she told me that he was still in South Africa and working as a judge. She'll go back there for a while when she's out of hospital, but their relationship is international; they see each other twice a year. She works over here as a lawyer and plans to head back home permanently in ten years when she's gained all the experience she needs to start her own law firm. Now, that is commitment. And no more unconventional than me and Alison not being together very long when she got pregnant.

I asked Marge about religion as I saw she had a little Bible with her and she explained that she would be introducing her son to the church because she wanted him to have a moral code and know right from wrong. I'm fairly sure that we don't need church for this, but I listened nonetheless. Marge explained that the comfort of having God in someone's life can bring them out of loneliness and stop them being scared. I suppose that she's right, it is good for that. It's something to think about. I'm not sure it'll change my opinion, though. I think it'd be better to let Charlie make his own mind up about stuff like that. If me and Alison don't go about the place coveting our neighbours or killing any sheep then he should be able to gain a sense of right and wrong from our actions, surely?

As I was putting the birth certificate back into the folder that the hospital gives you all the birth documents in, I saw there were vouchers galore, everything from nappies to formula to holidays and clothing. I wish I'd seen this when I was looking for new babygros on Charlie's first day.

There was also a number to call for a proper photographer to come to the ward and take a picture. I was a bit put off by this at first. It seemed a bit unsavoury, but then I suppose it's a good business idea for someone ... who doesn't want a professional photo of their newborn?

A couple who have fathers with huge cameras, that's who.

Alison woke up before Charlie and I held him while she went for a shower. She's still having to wear the special maternity pants that they gave her, and she's still sore. She hobbled back from the shower, bless her. She is so strong and inspiring. I'd be moaning like high hell if it was me that was in the pain that she clearly is. She isn't even allowed any decent painkillers as she is breastfeeding. Just paracetamol, really. I did ask the midwife while Alison was in the shower if she'd be allowed gas and air, but she confirmed that this was just for the birth and not for 'enjoyment'. She must have thought I was asking for it for myself. Alison returned from the shower looking radiant. There was something about her I hadn't noticed while she was lying in bed in a nightgown, I suppose the sweat and tied back hair stood in the way of her true beauty. She had the glow of someone special. At that moment I realised, again, just how lucky I am to have her in my life. I was also lucky as Charlie had just shit himself and needed changing. Unfortunately for me, it leaked out the side and down my T-shirt a bit. I had a choice to make; wear something of Alison's or the hospital's, or walk to the car like a top off chav, not an easy decision for anyone to make. I ended up leaving there and then, it was just before main visitors' time and I thought I could get to the car before anyone saw me. This I managed. Driving home with the smell of baby poo in the car, though, was something different altogether. I struggled to not add an adult's sick to my T-shirt's absorbent abilities.

I had a bag of dirty babygros with me that Alison had given me to wash, so once I was home they, along with my T-shirt and everything else I was wearing, went into the machine on the hottest temperature with double the amount of tablets I'd normally use. Then it was time to thoroughly scrub my hands and fingernails with the washing up brush. It's unbelievable how aggressive baby poo is when it comes to sticking to a human. My hands looked like I'd been making baby poo sandwiches and all I'd done was handle babygros and my T-shirt as they went into the machine. I'm going to have to buy some rubber gloves and keep them for such emergencies. By all accounts this is just the beginning of things to come.

I headed back to the hospital. When I arrived the midwife was waiting for me. She said that Alison was doing well, although I needed to also learn how to feed the baby. She must have seen the panicked look on my face as I looked down at my chest and felt for my non-existent man breasts. 'No, no, I mean with a bottle. I'll be along in a bit to show you, if you'd like to learn?' she offered.

Of course, the one time I didn't want a member of the NHS staff to turn up on time, she did. Anne, as I learned her name was, didn't waste any time in scooping Charlie up and placing him, screaming, into my arms before she got busy with a tiny little bottle of formula that she must have had in her pocket, as it just appeared from nowhere.

The lesson was OK, Anne was very knowledgeable, but I fear that when the time comes for me to do it on my own, I'll mess it up. Charlie didn't really seem like he wanted the bottle at first and I was all for giving up and letting him wait until he was hungry, but Anne reminded me that he probably doesn't know he's hungry at the moment, all he knows is that something isn't right, so when the time comes that he needs food he'll scream and scream, working himself up into one so much that he won't be able to calm down enough to get the milk down him. So keeping that in mind I carefully guided the teat of the bottle into his mouth and after a while he opened his eyes, tried to focus, probably couldn't, closed them again and began to drink the milk. I was feeding my son.

It felt great.

Thursday September 27th 2012

I was on the ward today, watching Alison and the midwife feeding Charlie. Alison seems to be getting the hang of things now and Charlie is not spitting out his milk straight away. He is sometimes taking a bottle and at other times just having breast milk. Anyway, Marge, the woman who was in the next bed, has taken herself and little Jonathon home, so there is a new and much more mental woman in the next bed now. She's had twins. The husband has his work cut out. I'm not sure where she came from, but it seems she's been in hospital for a while. She definitely moved from another bed, as through the curtain this afternoon we could hear her moaning that someone had stolen the five quid credit off her TV package from the other bed. She was demanding that her husband go and ask whoever was in her old bed to cough up a fiver. Her husband wasn't keen on asking an either heavily pregnant woman or new mother to give him five pounds on the off chance that it was her that used up the credit on the tele.

I'm fairly sure the woman had some issues, as she started saying things like, 'Well, if it was me, I'd use it, but I don't think people should be able to get away with it. She's been caught, fair cop.' When her husband tried to get firm with her and tell her he wasn't doing it, she changed tack and got all manipulative about it. 'Why don't you go over and say, did you enjoy the film? We've watched it as well and would like to thank you for ordering it on our credit.' Her husband wandered off, promising to have a look and see who was in her old bed. He walked past our bed; I wanted to give him a look of solidarity, but he avoided eye contact. He looked like he was too busy looking at the floor, concentrating on at what point exactly he'd made the wrong decision that ended him up going to ask someone in hospital for his five pounds back. I could hear him talking to one of the midwives in the corridor explaining his wife's concerns.

He returned not more than two minutes later saying that it looked like the woman was about to be taken into the delivery room. I don't know why he even went and looked, if it had been me I'd have just walked to the end of the ward and back and then told Alison that no one was in the bed and held my hands up in an 'I tried' kind of way. He didn't, though, he was honest and I blame him for the next two hours of moaning, crying and despair we had to listen to from the love of his life. I wanted to go and give her a fiver just to stop the noise. Alison wouldn't let me, though. I can see why, it was clear after about half an hour that the TV was not the issue, the woman was a class A nutter and didn't care who heard about it. I just thanked my lucky stars that Alison was not like her.

I took Charlie for a little walk around the ward, not that there was far to go, but I wasn't allowed to take him to the café, so it was just up and down the corridor and then we sat together in the family room for a while until it was visiting time and loads of big brothers and sisters of all the other new babies came in and wanted to watch TV. One young lad, he must have been about six or seven, wanted to look at Charlie. He then said, 'I've got a little sister, can we swap? I wanted a brother.'

I replied 'How much will you give me?' which I thought would make him laugh, but he put in a firm offer of everything in his piggybank and his twenty-four hour La Mans Scalextric set. I decided it was time to go and wake Alison up then. Besides which, Charlie gets quite heavy to hold after a while.

I got back to the bed and Alison's parents were there, ready and waiting for their turn to hold Charlie. Of course, my parents were in the café waiting for their own turn. Bill informed us that yesterday they'd not been able to get a photo of the grandparents together as the women had gone in first, then the men, rather than grandmother and grandfather. I left them to it and went to the café to see what mum would buy me for lunch: a pasty and oil-soaked chips, it turned out.

I went home this afternoon after lunch and let Alison's mum stay with her. I was feeling tired and I needed to get a few items out of boxes, which in the end I forgot to do. I slept from 4 p.m. until eight. I woke up in a panic, thinking that Alison would have been trying to get hold of me, but checking my phone I could see she hadn't. I phoned her and asked if she was OK; she was just about to give Charlie his last feed and get some sleep, I asked if she needed anything, but she had everything, her mum had just left. My parents had been in and out, too. She said I needed my sleep and told me not to worry about coming up. This panicked me as I was unsure if this was something I'd be able to live with myself over. Alison was quite sure, though, and didn't sound annoyed at all.

I was going to go back to sleep, but I think the instant worry that came on produced so much adrenaline that I couldn't have even if I'd wanted to. I ended up unpacking everything that needed unpacking and putting together all that needed to be put together. The cot took a while to do on my own, but it was my fault for not looking at the instructions. I didn't realise it would be so hard, but once I'd finished and it was still wobbling like some old drunk, I knew it wasn't right. I ended up having to fish the instructions out of the recycling bin outside that I'd chucked everything in once I'd unpacked.

All this was done with intermediate checking of my phone as I went along. There weren't any messages, but I did find myself opening the photo app every time and looking at the picture I had of my little man.

He's great, I can't wait to see what we're going to end up doing together. I hope he has the same interests as me. Not that I don't want him to bond with Alison, but I would like to have the father-son thing that women don't understand – the one that isn't screaming and shouting at each other. When I was a kid I used to like putting models together and then stringing the planes from the ceiling on fishing wire. I hope Charlie has some interest in that. It's all computers these days, but I can't see how a virtual version of that would be much fun.

I thought about watching a film, but I've been writing this for almost an hour and I haven't been focusing on what the film is about – I couldn't even tell you who the main character is – so with that I'm going to bed. Hopefully I'll be able to bring my son home tomorrow.

Friday September 28th 2012

I brought my son home today. When I got to the hospital both mother and baby were asleep. The mad lady with the twins was singing along to the theme tune from the news and her husband was just sitting staring down the corridor, looking absolutely shattered. I'm glad I haven't got twins and a mad wife to take home, he's probably having anxiety attacks just thinking about what it will be like with no nurses or midwives around to help him.

Charlie screamed all the way from the ward to the car and continued screaming while I made a complete hash of getting the car seat strapped in. I should have practised it. I even told Alison that I had practised it. I hadn't though, when it came to it, I always found something better to do. The task was made harder by Charlie screaming right into my ear the whole time. I don't think the makers of the seats have parents in mind when they design them. You have to lean over the seat to plug the belt in, then go back on yourself to wrap one part of the belt around the back and then the other goes over the front of the seat into little fiddly clips, although I think I must have a defective one, as the belt wouldn't come out any further, so the part that was supposed to go across the back just lay over the hood of the chair. It was OK, though, because Alison didn't see it.

Charlie screamed all the way out of the car park, too, but once on the open road he dropped off. I couldn't see he'd dropped off as the seat looks the other way, he'd just stopped crying so we assumed he had. We then pulled over in a layby to check he hadn't died. He hadn't; he screamed when I got out and walked round to look, so we drove on until the next time Alison thought it would be a good idea for me to get out into the rain and check he was still breathing. He was. Three further times I had to stop and check. I should have asked her to get in the back where she could see him, but I'd dumped all the bags, towels, nappies and everything else I'd carried out to the car there and didn't want to have to move it to the boot in the rain.

At home things felt strange. We had Charlie there. We had no idea what to do, so Alison got him out the car seat and sat down while I went and made us a drink. By the time I got back they were both asleep, Charlie spread out on Alison and Alison spread out on the sofa. I took a picture and went off to find somewhere to sit.

Must remember to buy another chair.

I've got to properly give up smoking now. Charlie is home and I can't be smelling like an ash tray with him here. The health visitor is coming round tomorrow, I can't be stinking of smoke when she gets here, either. I need to make the decision and follow through with the action. It's just too nice, though.

Saturday September 29th 2012

Yesterday didn't turn out to be the peaceful day it seemed it would be. I'd just about sat down (on the edge of the bed) when the door went; it was my parents to see the new bundle of joy in our lives. My parents came in, as did Alison's, and at one point me, Dad and Bill were gathered on the landing while all the ladies changed Charlie in the bedroom. No one stayed long, although I think they would have liked to have done … but neither set of parents wanted to put out the other one and they realised that there were probably too many people in the house. They left after promising to let each other know when they were going to be coming so as not to crowd little Charlie.

Later Keith came round with Lauren, his girlfriend. I haven't met her before, but she seems his normal type. Bit fat, actually. Nice enough to talk to, though, and they'd actually bought a gift, which means Lauren must be a good person because there's no way that Keith would have thought to buy it himself. He'd have thought giving us one of his brothers' or sisters' teddy bears, which he had done before the birth, was more than enough. He'd have just turned up and tried to force money on us. They hung around for a bit while Alison tried to unsuccessfully calm Charlie down. I felt a bit rude because by the time they left I'd stopped talking and had taken to staring at the wall, silently wishing they'd leave. It didn't stop me saying, 'Oh, no. Don't be silly, stay' when Keith said that they could see we had other things to do. I'm not sure why I did it, because I'd been thinking about just telling them to get out. Not that I wanted to be rude, but because I was so tired and fed up hearing the screaming that I couldn't take anything else into my brain.

When Alison's friend Catherine and her partner turned up within twenty minutes of Keith and Lauren leaving, I was close to breaking point. The smile still plastered on my face must have made me seem like a mental case. I'd gone into mania. It was a relief to see that there were only a few nappies left in the packet as I led Catherine and her extremely tall partner into the bedroom, where Alison was now receiving guests.

I went for a walk. It wasn't really a walk I was going for, or nappies. I was going out to buy some cigarettes and I knew it. I hadn't planned to buy any today; when I woke up I decided I was going to see if I could get through the day without any, but I only bought ten, ten lovely Benson and Hedges. I thought I'd really enjoy the hit of nicotine on the back of my throat, but instead I had a coughing fit when I inhaled the sulphur from the match I lit it with. I persevered, though, and soon felt the benefit. A lung full of lovely tobacco smoke and a head full of nothing other than the thousands of toxins that cigarettes contain.

When I got home Catherine and Mr Tall were just getting ready to leave. After the longest goodbye in the world, they finally left. I asked Alison if she'd felt stressed with all the visits, too, and she had, so we've decided to only see one set of visitors per day. I've made a sign to put on the door after the first people have been. It says:

'Thanks for coming, we are all OK, but tired. We'll be in touch very soon. Thanks, Graham, Alison and Charlie.

P.S. If you're the health visitor, please knock.'

I got the idea out of my book. I'm sure they wouldn't put it in a book if people were likely to be upset when they read it.

The first night was pretty much a nightmare (for Alison). I slept through most of the crying, apparently. Charlie was up for most of the night, though. He slept for about an hour, then wanted feeding so woke up again and it was like that all night. It's been like it all day, too.

I feel helpless, Diary. All I can do is change his nappy and just about feed him a bottle, but most of what he needs at the moment is from his mum.

I've smoked all the cigs I bought, too, I was only planning on having one a night after we'd sorted little Charlie out of an evening, but after 5 p.m. I decided that the health visitor wasn't coming anyway, so I'd be OK to just crack on and smoke them.

Alison was worried that the health visitor hadn't come. She's managed to feed and change Charlie all day … well, apart from the one time that I did it (really well) so we've not struggled too much. I understand why she's worried, though, she needs reassurance that she's doing the right thing and that she's not doing any harm. It doesn't matter who tells her she's doing great, she needs to hear it from a professional. It's a natural new mother's fear, I should think. The more I tried to comfort her, the more Alison worried that the health visitor hadn't come when she said she was going to as she was waiting for Social Services to come with her. I assured her that there was no need for Social Services to come and see what we were up to, and besides which, the health visitor works for the NHS, so there is nothing unusual about her not being somewhere she said she was going to be or not doing something she said she would do.

Alison decided that she'd ring the health visitor, Lynette, and check, but there was no response, the phone just rang and rang. She was no doubt out on the piss. Whenever there's *'If we don't get time, we'll come the next day'* added to any sentence, they might as well just say, *'Look, it's Saturday, we don't really care so we'll see you at the latest possible time we can get away with.'*

One day when I'm rich I'm going to get us private health care. Mark my words, Diary, if there is ever a political party that has the balls to come out and say the NHS is going and all the national insurance we pay will stop and go into health insurance funds instead, I'll be voting for them no matter who they are.

Sunday September 30th 2012

I was up all night last night, I wanted to be supportive and I didn't want Alison to tell her mates that I was no help, so every time she was feeding Charlie, I went and got her a snack or a drink or something. The book told me to do the little things that I can and all I can think of at the moment is making her food and drink. I change him, but Alison seems to like doing that, too. She's a great mum and has taken to it like a duck to water. She soothes Charlie just by holding him and seems to have a sixth sense when it comes to what he wants. I feel less than useful; I can't even remember to wash my hands in between changing him and making Alison a sandwich. I hope she's not ill. I'm not and I licked the butter from my fingers, so hopefully she'll be OK.

I haven't told her about it yet, there's no point in worrying her. I will go out and buy some proper antibacterial hand wash as soon as possible. I've seen my dad use it in the garden. He carries it round on a belt loop. I don't think I'll go that far, but I might leave it on the little shelf near the bedroom door.

In between making dirty snacks for Alison, I paced the house, moved things about from one place to another, and tried to read my baby book. I'm going to try and have a sleep this afternoon. The sign is going back up. Alison is also sleeping whenever she can, so I'll put my head down when they do.

6.00 p.m.

No word from the health visitor today, either. Alison rang her again and left another message.

7.30 p.m.

Lynette phoned and said that she'd been ill this weekend and wouldn't be able to make it round until tomorrow. She had hoped that bank staff would have been arranged, but found out they hadn't when she checked her phone this evening. This is what annoys me about the NHS, the people that work for it are all nice people … well, the lower level guys, the ones on the frontline are, but as soon as you get above them it's full of lazy, there-for-the-money, arseholes. There just isn't sufficient money to have enough people on the ground doing the work that needs doing. Of course, this doesn't stop the managers and the directors taking fat pay checks, which they justify by harping on that they'd earn double that in the private sector. Well, they might, but they'd have to spend most of it on educating themselves to the level of whatever it is they do, so when you work it all out there isn't really a huge difference.

Lynette promised to come round tomorrow first thing. I'm not sure if she heard me shouting in the background about a complaint form or not. it is so frustrating that we're brought up to believe that we've got the best health service in the world and that people should consider themselves lucky, but when you actually need it, it's a different story and just a massive pain in the arse. I've said it before, and I'll no doubt say it again. The problem is zero accountability, or a lack of it, anyway. I'm fairly sure if there are bonuses to be had the figures are all just made up anyway, and the government will allow that as they don't like to look like they're in charge of a shitty operation.

Maybe I should just write a letter of complaint. I'm sure I've written more than one letter's worth about my complaints with them.

9.30 p.m.

I woke up to a text from my mother.

'Don't you want people to meet with Charlie? I brought Aunty Joan round today, but your rude sign made it clear you didn't want visitors so we left. Joan has gone home now, she'll see Charlie next summer.'

This is bad, Joan lives right on the border of England and Scotland. I didn't know she was coming or I'd have taken the sign down.

I rang Mum later and explained. She was frosty to begin with, but when I told her I'd got the idea out of a book and not thought it up myself to keep her away, she eased up. I've promised to send Joan a thank you card for the teddy and cheque she left for Charlie.

I felt guilty this evening when I was holding Charlie. Aunty Joan has always, without fail, sent me money on Christmas and birthdays and has been far more interested in my dull life than most people in the family. I rang her up and told her to turn her computer on. We then had a video chat and I introduced her to Charlie over Skype. She was happy and agreed that he was a handsome little devil. She told me off in an Aunty type way for calling Charlie a little chimpanzee.

She is going to come down and see him in the New Year. By the time the call ended, she was fine with me and understood why I'd put the sign up. I couldn't say goodbye properly as Charlie did a tremendous trump and filled his nappy. Joan even heard the noise it made in Scotland, albeit over Skype.

I texted my mum back after the call and let her know I'd spoken to Joan. She didn't reply; I suppose it's late, though.

OCTOBER 2012

Monday October 1st 2012

Mum texted at 4.30 a.m. I didn't know she got up so early, or checked her phone as soon as she did. She was fine with my explanation and even apologised for not letting us know she was popping round with Aunty Joan.

We had no plans today. I left the sign up and tried to get a lie in; it's not easy though, Charlie is asleep more than he is awake, but he does wake up regularly to either fill his nappy or have some food. There is little else he can do; at the moment it's just nature running his every move.

Lynette, the health visitor, turned up this afternoon at about three, and she looked like death. I did my bit and made her a honey and lemon drink, although I didn't have any honey so I just used sugar. She did all the checks on Charlie, checking that he didn't have any marks on him and that Alison was feeding him correctly. The main thing Lynette says we need to remember is not to force him to feed, as he'll let us know by crying if he hasn't had enough/needs feeding in the first place. She checked that he wasn't harmed at all and gave him a little weighing. He has lost a pound, but that is normal apparently. I don't know if the gunk he had all over him when they weighed him the first time weighed a lot, but Lynette wasn't concerned. She didn't stay long, just long enough to give us all the details of where she would be this week. She's given us her personal number, just in case no one else comes at the end of the week as they should. Lynette will be ringing in sick this week. It's a sad state of affairs when someone doesn't have the backing of their employers at all and has to leave their sick bed.

She had no concerns over Charlie or Alison, though, and was out the house long before her sugar and lemon water had gone cold. I only saw her take a sip, too. Ungrateful would be one word I'd think of.

Charlie is sleeping well through the day. Mind you, he sleeps well most of the time, although just for short periods. My book says there is nothing you can do about this, other than focus on the magic three month period when things like sleep should get better. Everywhere I'm hearing about this three month period: books, magazines, the Internet, from other people, they're all on about it. It's like something special just happens at that point. It's the point at which most people recognise a baby as not being a complete and utter nightmare. It seems so far away, though.

I've found myself smoking more, not less. It's a reason to go outside. Alison isn't happy about it and makes me shower when I come back in, but to be honest, regular showers are stopping my eyes burning from tiredness.

I'm not sure if I ever thought looking after a baby and new

mum would be easy, I think it's more a case that I just never thought about it at all. I never needed to. Having Charlie has changed me already. I went out to buy more cigs today and in the shop there was a young mum having a nightmare with a toddler. Before I'd have judged her for not being able to keep her kid under control. Today I felt a solidarity with her, I felt her pain. I don't think I could have dealt with babies when I was younger. As I was walking home, I hoped that she wasn't on her own, it'd be even harder with no one to share the burden.

When I got home, Charlie was screaming for his dinner, Alison looked so tired, and there was nothing I could do about it. It makes me feel helpless. Charlie just wants milk, he doesn't want me pulling faces at him trying to make him smile weeks before it's possible for him to do so. He wouldn't latch onto Alison's nipple and it made him scream more, he's not able to understand that the reason he can't latch on is because he's screaming, so he screams more because he's not getting what he wants. I couldn't do anything, so I went for what seemed like the hundredth shower of the day. I had to use Alison's shampoo instead of my normal manly Lynx. I knew I shouldn't have washed my hair every time I showered.

In the shower, I was thinking about work; I would have been there today if I wasn't on paternity leave. I thought about Boris's normal Monday routine, stumbling about near the sink, and the bets me and the chef had on what time he would be either sick or open the cooking wine. I've hated work for as long as I can remember, it's something I've always put myself through. I've never really been one for phoning in sick that much; this pregnancy aside, I don't think I've done it when I've not been sick before. I thought it meant that it was because I was so committed to Alison and Charlie. Thinking about it now, though, I think it's just that I dislike the boss more than I have in any other job I've had. When I was at the bus depot, where most of them took the piss out of me, it was bad, but at least there they knew when to stop. With Jane it's horrible, she's so inconsistent in her behaviour, one day I'm flavour of the month, another it's like I've stolen her personal belongings and need punishing for it.

There's no doubt about it, I need to plan a career out. One that isn't physical labour, I think. I've worked my fingers to the bone enough over the last fifteen years. I think I've earned a bit of pencil pushing and people talking. I bet if I were to get my dream job of working in a homeless hostel I wouldn't have to wash up more than a couple of cups a few times a week. There'd be no dodging chef's violent outbursts and no Boris talking to me under the partition in the toilet when I'm taking an unofficial break. I don't think anyone else in any job does that, though, it's just Boris and his funny ways.

Or maybe there's a Boris in all jobs. I don't remember there being a crazy Russian in any of the other jobs I had, though, although I do remember when I worked in the bus depot, there was a guy that used to drive the number sixty-seven into town. He used to talk to no one but the passengers, which is weird in itself, but he only used to say three things: 'Hello'; 'safe journey'; and 'ta-ta'. That was it. No one else ever heard a peep out of him. Even his boss got nothing more than grunts and groans on top of his three word repertoire. I suppose there are just some right weirdos in this world and the best any of us can hope for is that it isn't us.

Wednesday October 3rd 2012

Mum was round today, she'd decided it was time for Charlie's first bath. The poor little sod looked terrified as she lowered him in, with me and Alison peering over the edge of the tub. Once he was in and Mum had her hand behind his head, he seemed to relax a little. I've read that babies like baths as it reminds them of when they were inside their mother's womb. I'm sure if he was able to, he would have smiled while in there.

He didn't like getting out, though, not one bit. Once we'd just sponged him down (you're not allowed to use soap on babies) Mum lifted him out and the cold air hit him. He let us know this was not to his liking and Alison got his little towel around him quickly.

I must say he seemed very relaxed once we'd got him back into his warm clothes again.

Monday October 8th 2012

Time seems to have changed. I don't mean moved forward like it always does, I mean I don't seem to have a day and night anymore. Time is sectioned into feeding time and not feeding time. Whether it's day or night doesn't seem to matter. I'm not back at work until next week so that doesn't even break up the day and let my body know when it's time to sleep and when it should be awake. I'm constantly tired.

Alison doesn't seem to be as knackered as me … she must be, though. Maybe I just talk about it too much.

Charlie certainly has a brand new set of lungs. He's been screaming a lot today, I don't think we're moving fast enough for him at times; when he's hungry, he wants feeding – there is no time for getting ready or moving him from one room to the other. It's not just crying, he actually screams … screams like he's being murdered. When he really gets going there's no consoling him. The noise he makes is fairly terrible. I read that it's nature's way of making sure a baby's needs do not go unmet. I'd say nature has done a cracking job on that. Nature truly is a bastard, that's all I can say.

Wednesday October 10th 2012

Charlie is waking up every hour, feeding and then going back to sleep. I've checked my book and it seems this is normal. I thought babies were supposed to stay awake for a bit. The only time he wakes up other than that is when we change him. He certainly wakes up then. Not only does he wake up, he lets us know he's awake and not happy about it.

Our sleep pattern is not something a doctor would recommend.

Thursday October 11th 2012

Charlie has started to tell us he's hungry by sucking his hand. It's crazy. I must have a really intelligent son for him to be able to communicate with us before he's three weeks old.

Saturday October 13th 2012

Lynette popped round today and I told her enthusiastically about Charlie sucking his hand. She tried to tell me it was common and all babies did it, but I could tell she was impressed at the level of learning my son has.

She checked him out physically, made sure there wasn't any

cigarette burns on him or anything, and then did all the normal medical things, like checking his pulse. It would appear that as well as having an intelligently advanced son, he is also the picture of health. Maybe even a medical marvel.

He can scream though; boy, can he scream.

It's the last time we'll see Lynette, so we're on our own from here on in. It feels liberating, but it's also scary as hell. Alison made sure she had a direct number for Lynette before she unlocked the front door and allowed her to leave.

I hope we'll be OK. I didn't let on to Alison that I'm as terrified as her.

Sunday October 14th 2012

Charlie was screaming uncontrollably for three hours last night. It was a relief when he passed out from exhaustion, although being the fit young baby he is, he was awake again within half an hour and screaming for another two. He only stopped when all the screaming caused him to fill his nappy and babygro with the worst kind of chicken korma-looking poo imaginable; it smelled horrendous.

As Alison had been holding him for the last hour of his outburst I agreed to change him, I thought that the best thing to do would be to pop him straight in the baby bath and undress him in there. It wasn't the best idea I've ever had, but as there was poo everywhere I thought it would be a good idea to contain it in something I could pressure wash in the garden later. Charlie didn't like the baby bath with no water in, though. The plastic was a bit cold, but I think if I ask him when he's a bit older he'll agree that he did over react somewhat. In the end I carried him up the stairs naked and got him wrapped in a towel and waited for the adult size bath to run, then I bathed him. It hurt my back no end as you can't really put babies in the bath and leave them, you have to hold them so they don't slip down and drown. That's rule number one in the parenting handbook: don't kill your children.

Alison came in and took him to get changed as, if I'm hard on myself, I was making a bit of a pig's ear of things and Charlie was screaming again. He stopped as soon as he was in Alison's arms. Which didn't make me feel great.

I thought the first bath I gave him would be great and filled with bubble bath fun. It wasn't, though. It had screaming, splashing and me cleaning the bath out after he pooed in it.

Monday October 15th 2012

I went back to work today. After being full of fear through the night about being tired, it turned out I was tired. It's funny how when you're worried about being tired, it becomes a self-fulfilling prophecy.

Jane was in but she didn't talk much, she just put me straight on washing up. There's a new timetable now. It seems she's worked out my plan of getting off the fryer on Fridays and has stuck me on there. The whole week is planned out to be as bad as it can be. I didn't think she knew all my little tricks, but it seems she does. Washing up on a Monday is always bad as the guys that work weekends leave the last serving's worth of plates. They're also pretty rubbish at their jobs, so most things need doing again before chef can use them.

I thought about moaning, but then decided I wouldn't give her the satisfaction of hearing it, and just got on with it.

Boris seemed pleased to see me; he wanted to know why I hadn't rung him and shared the news. I reminded him we weren't actually friends, but he didn't listen and just moved the conversation on to the baby's name. Of course, he thought I'd done Charlie some damage by not naming him Boris, but he conceded during toilet break that Charlie was a good name as many British kings had been called Charles. I left my cubicle as Boris was listing all the Russian tsars called, you guessed it, Boris. I doubt he even noticed I'd gone he was so engrossed in his own story.

The afternoon was more of the same, Jane had me on deliveries, which meant I had to carry all the oil and bags of heavy stuff up three flights of stairs to the store. As I was getting the first load, I could hear Jane talking to the delivery driver. She said, 'Yeah, well, it's nice to be the boss of people, I wouldn't get out of bed for less than thirty grand these days, ha ha.' I'm not sure if she expected the driver to believe that as the manager of a small kitchen in a department store she was earning that, but I know it isn't true. The warehouse managers don't even earn that. I decided I would just look at the funny side of things; here was Jane, the person who caused me the most anxiety, trying to impress a driver with lies about how much she earned. She must really hate herself to have to invent someone she isn't to tell others about.

Tuesday October 16th 2012

Today was more of the same: screaming, screaming, screaming, pass out, more screaming, big explosive poo and then OK for a while. I did what I could, but it turns out there's little I can do to help. The screaming has started to go through me; I struggle to be able to cope. Charlie has the ability to position his head right next to my ear when he is in fifth gear and there's no consoling the poor little blighter.

I've found myself more and more often giving him back to Alison when he is screaming.

I hope this doesn't mean I'm a terrible father.

Wednesday October 17th 2012

We took Charlie to the doctor today. The screaming hadn't stopped for hours and after a 3 a.m. phone call to the maternity ward, only to be told it's normal, we were first in the queue at the surgery this morning. The screaming is so bad we think he must be ill. Getting him ready to travel was something of a mission. First we had to dress him in his thick clothes. Charlie doesn't like this, it annoys him. The trousers were OK but when we were getting his arms into the sleeves of the jumper was when he really started protesting. We managed in the end, though, then it was into the car seat and in the car. He fell asleep on the journey, which is something I need to remember. All too soon we arrived and Charlie woke up as soon as I opened the door.

Being in the waiting room with a screaming baby is a terrible experience; you can feel everyone's eyes looking at you, judging you as bad parents. It does help you to be seen quickly, though. Normally, regardless of turning up for your appointment on time, you're in for an hour's wait at our doctors; today we were seen within ten minutes and five of them were before our appointment time.

To say the doctor was helpful would be a drastic

overstatement. He wasn't. All he did was undress Charlie (cue more screaming) then give him the once over with a cold stethoscope and tell us it was colic. That was it. No medicine, no advice, just that it was colic and that he'd grow out of it. I asked how long that would take and he shrugged his shoulders and informed us some babies have it for up to six months, but not to worry because it was normal.

That was it. We carried a still-screaming baby out of the surgery and back to the car. Charlie was asleep within five minutes, so I kept driving; we went around the country lanes for an hour and a half and only returned as I felt faint and needed some food.

Charlie was OK for a little while in the afternoon, but come teatime he was back to his screaming.

I phoned my mum and she said that it's normally wind that causes problems with young babies. She suggested something called gripe water. This is apparently what I was given when I had wind. I went out to get some. The chemist charged over seven quid for the biggest bottle, but I thought if it's going to work, then why not put it on the credit card?

Getting it into the baby was another nightmare all of its own. He's too young to know how to use a spoon and we're too clumsy to know how to not pour a spoonful of gripe water over his face. This wasn't helpful. It's my fault for thinking that the gripe water would be like medicine, rather than water. It wasn't though. It was like water. The second go wasn't much better. I know it's supposed to stop them screaming, but I don't think it's meant to be because they're scared to put it in their mouths, so they shut up shop as soon as they see the spoon coming toward them. Alison suggested a syringe, although I didn't have any of them and it was too late to go and get one. I ended up sucking a bit of gripe water into a straw that I had left over from KFC and holding the fluid in it with some superior sucking skills; then, when Charlie opened his mouth to scream, I gently eased up on the pressure and the fluid fell into his mouth. I definitely didn't do as Alison accused me of and blow the gripe water down the back of his throat. It was his fault he coughed as he was just sucking air in for a loud scream. He was shocked to find that there was gripe water where the air should have been and wriggled a bit before swallowing. Then he just looked at me with his big brown eyes, not quite sure what to do. So he had a paddy anyway. Thankfully it didn't last long, though, as we were able to calm him with a little walk around the house. He burped as we were on the second lap of the kitchen. I think that's just what he needed.

Thursday October 18th 2012

More of the same. We've ordered something called 'Clife' from America. It cost $19.99 and the shipping was free if you wanted to wait until next year to get it. We didn't, so have paid for overnight express shipping, and it should be here by Saturday.

Later I drove round the town, going into five different chemists and listening to five different opinions on what a) causes colic and b) treats it. It's funny how it's always the expensive thing that the actual pharmacist recommends, but the assistants are more than happy to agree that the doctors are rubbish and give you a bit of honest advice. I've got some gripe water, some more drops, a book and one maniac even gave me the card of an osteopath, although what she was thinking I don't know, maybe when I'd said 'baby screaming', she'd heard 'back hurting'.

Friday October 19th 2012

Early this morning I was lying in my bed when Alison brought Charlie in. He was looking about and wasn't in pain. It's moments of calmness like this that remind me it's not all bad. Alison went for a shower, which left Charlie chilling out in his U-shaped pillow on the bed with me, his little bare feet poking out of his tiny trousers. I was playing with him, just touching his nose and moving my hand around, keeping his eyes following it, and when I ran my finger across his top lip, he smiled. It was a faint one, but he definitely smiled. He held my gaze as he did it and I could see the happiness in his eyes. I got over excited and tried to tickle his feet and make him do it again, but this was probably too much for him and he started to cry until I picked him up and took him over to the window. He loves looking out the window, I think he finds it therapeutic. That and water; he'll watch someone drink and, if you're holding him when you turn the tap on, he is fixated on the water running down. I might get one of those 1980s indoor water features: it might calm him down.

Alison was upset that she'd missed the smile, so upset that she started pretending that she had seen him do it before. I don't like to call anyone a liar, but I could see in her face that she was making it up. She took him away and lay him on the mat in the living room and I could hear her trying to make him smile. After about ten minutes of feeling uncomfortable and worrying that I'd harmed Alison, I heard her shrill with delight. I went down and there was Charlie looking up at his mum with a big smile on his face. It was like it was glued on. I made sure

Alison knew it was bigger than the one that I'd got, and she didn't get all smug like I had, she just allowed me to share the moment with them. I think this is where men and women are different. We tend to think that everything is a competition, whereas women see it as a game to be enjoyed. It's the same with Monopoly. Unfortunately I had to go to work and leave mother and son looking at each other, so I couldn't stay and work out how to win.

Work was the normal Friday. I was moved onto the washing up within an hour of being there for dishing up raw bacon 'by mistake'. Jane put Boris on the grill/fryer, but come eleven, when it was time for the fish to be fried and the mess to be made, she moved me back. This was without Boris being an idiot and breaking anything, she just decided to move me back on the fryer. I think she might have rumbled my game. She then took Boris off somewhere; we were all hoping it was to HR to have him sacked for being the drunk mess he is at work, but within twenty minutes they were both back. They must have been unloading a big order as they looked worn out.

I had to stay behind today to clean up the mess I made with the batter. Jane also asked me to clean the fryer. I agreed I would, but as soon as she'd left with everyone else I decided I wouldn't be doing that. As long as the kitchen was clean, I was happy; there was no way I was cutting into any more of my weekend by cleaning out a dirty fryer that Boris could have done in the time we are paid to work if he hadn't been in the storeroom drinking the cooking sherry. I'm fairly sure Jane was in there having a drink with him as the door was shut for ages and they both came out looking red-faced and rosy-cheeked.

I went the long way home, via town. I thought I might be able to find Charlie a water feature. There weren't any in the old Woolworths shop, which was taken over by the staff that had worked in it before Woolies went bust. It's now called Wellworths, but it wasn't well worth anything; I couldn't see anything that made being in there worth it at all. I suppose it's a sign of British stamina that they managed to get it all set up, though; well, that and the fact that all they had to do to the uniforms was change a couple of letters on the badge. Then they just replaced all the Woolworths branded stock, paid Woolworths off with a few quid, and got themselves on the news as some proper British go-getters.

I looked in a couple more shops on the way home. The only places that had them were Argos (way too expensive) and dodgy Michael on the market, who has stock that looks like he owns a key to the back door of Argos, incidentally. No one local buys from him as it's well known that anything you buy could be taken back by the police and you charged with handling stolen goods. I don't know how he is still trading.

I bought Alison and Charlie a big smiley sunflower from one of the stalls in the market, as I thought it would be nice to mark the occasion of his first smiles with something smiley. It's a big one, probably double the size of Charlie. When I walked in the door with it, Charlie wasn't screaming, he was just finishing having some food, he looked up in shock at the sunflower, but then he gave a huge smile. Alison said he's been doing that all day, in between screaming like he's being beaten. Sure enough, within twenty minutes he'd started again and we had a poorly little boy to look after again.

By 7 p.m. it was time to put him down for the night. He'd cried himself to sleep in my arms. It's heartbreaking to see him in so much pain. He didn't wake up before I started writing this at 10 p.m. and hasn't until now, so maybe we're going to get a baby that sleeps through.

Alison went to bed at the same time Charlie went to sleep, I've got a bottle ready for when he wakes up. I doubt he'll take it, but at least I've tried to get her to sleep more. She can't, though, she has to get up and help him if she hears him screaming. It's inbuilt.

Saturday October 20th 2012

7.00 a.m.

We've been up since four. The screaming is immense, it's more than I can take. As well as Charlie screaming, Alison's still in pain; her stitches are itching and hurting her. Picking Charlie up hurts as it puts pressure on. I'm trying to do what I can, but Alison always tries to pick him up before I get there to help. We rang the number Lynette had left us at 6.30 a.m. and thankfully she answered, but she says all Alison can have is paracetamol as she's breastfeeding. Seems silly to me. I asked Alison if she thought stopping breastfeeding was a good idea if it meant she could get some better painkillers. She just shouted at me, though. Apparently she doesn't want Lynette to think she's doing anything but the right thing or she'll get grassed up to Social Services. I knew she'd listened too much to the propaganda at the antenatal classes. It's all Government-led to avoid people going to the doctors too much. It's a money saving exercise.

I asked Alison if Social Services has a crack team for babies that were not breastfed, but she didn't answer, she just hobbled off, telling Charlie that 'Daddy is a Silly Billy'.

It seems I am now being insulted, in baby talk, through the medium of talking to someone else.

Brilliant.

6.00 p.m.

The 'Clife' came via a courier this morning. It seems to have given us a little bit of peace this afternoon. I sent Alison to bed once Charlie had calmed down and seemed happy in my arms. Alison didn't sleep, but I suppose it was good that she got an hour's rest before he wanted feeding again and I became useless to him.

Monday October 22nd 2012

The screaming has started again. Gripe water doesn't work, 'Clife' doesn't work. The only thing that seems to do any good is sleep and I haven't been able to find a way of keeping a baby asleep for a long time. Not safely, anyway. There are all sorts of idiots online suggesting that giving your baby whisky or brandy will help them sleep. I'm fairly sure, though, that if Charlie's little stomach can't handle food yet, strong alcohol will make the problem worse, not better.

Jane put me on dishwasher duty today for no reason. I didn't mind doing it as a job, but I'm now wondering what the reason for it was. Boris was put on the till and within twenty minutes the queue was out the door while he struggled to remember which button opened the drawer. I think Jane is plotting something.

Wednesday October 24th 2012

Work was the normal grind today, filled with Jane moaning

and Boris talking drivel. He kept telling me who his favourite person in history called Boris is: it's the mayor of London. He's obsessed with London and his own name. I was glad when he went into the store room and didn't come out for an hour. It turns out the chef had closed the door behind him and instead of banging on the door to rouse some assistance, Boris decided that it would be a good time for a nap. So that's exactly what he did. It wasn't until Jane realised that she was soon going to have to start loading the dishwasher herself that she went looking for him. He'd been using a box of crisps as a pillow. We'll still sell the crisps though, Alien warlord, we'll still sell them. I bet you have better standards in your time.

I was pleased to get a photo on my phone from Alison of Charlie wrapped in his little bath towel. It has a hood for him too, he looked so cute.

When I got home, Alison was in a state. Charlie had been screaming all afternoon again. I held him for a while. Walking around with him didn't work, so I popped him in the car seat and went for a drive. I ended up at my parent's house, and they were only too happy to take him for a long walk in the new pram they'd bought for him. It seems that walking with him does the same as driving with him; this will save me some money in fuel.

I read my book while they were out walking. I learnt that babies don't know how to go to sleep. I think Charlie's mastered it, though: just scream and scream until you pass out. I might try it myself if he carries on.

My parents offered to have Charlie for the night this weekend. I'm going to ask Alison in the morning.

After I got home and we'd put him down, I started looking on the Internet for solutions again. There are endless remedies and potions that claim to help, so I decided to do a little more research this time as I think I could end up spending thousands trying to get Charlie better. Someone in America has even devised a 'medication-free way' of dealing with colic. I started to watch the video, but soon got bored. It was a hippy type person saying that his 'aura' wasn't right and that it needed aligning or something. Then she just started dancing with a baby that someone had been stupid enough to give her, and making weird noises. I think we'll give that one a miss, I hate the smell of joss sticks.

I've ordered some different drops to the last lot. They're called 'Colrel' and are to be dropped onto the nipples halfway through his feed. These ones are coming from the UK, though. I've paid next day postage, which is still expensive, but not as expensive as the stuff from the US.

I asked Alison if my parents could have Charlie while we went out for a meal or something. She was entirely against the idea. She said if my parents were to have him then hers would have to get a night, too, and she didn't want to give him away for two nights yet. She also reminded me that we don't have enough money to go out for meals. I don't feel so bad for trying out the new kebab shop on the way home the other day, now.

Thursday October 25th 2012

I know why Jane is so sympathetic to Boris now. She's bonking him. I was just going into the store to collect some sugar and there they were: at it. The dirty devils. Boris told me he was married. The image I've got in my head is dreadful.

There was an open bottle of cooking sherry on the shelf next to them.

I didn't leave straight away, as I imagine anyone else would have done. I got nervous and didn't know where to look. All I knew was that chef had sent me to get sugar and there were naked people in the way of that happening. It took Jane telling me to 'fucking get out' to snap me to my senses. I'm going to stop writing about it now as my brain keeps conjuring up images that I can't scrub away.

It was Charlie's one month birthday yesterday, but we both forgot. The month has gone so quickly, even though it seems like time slows to almost a stop when he is screaming. He'll be an all new kind of nightmare in no time. I'll have to move everything I own onto floating shelves out of harm's way.

Friday October 26th 2012

I rang in sick today, I just didn't have the strength to go in. Jane was still shouting when I hung up the phone. I hope that the college course comes and goes fast. I don't think I'm going to last in this job without telling her to shove it. She's become more and more mean towards me since I found her and Boris doing the dirty. I suppose now she feels threatened. I'm fairly sure she has a partner, too, so I suppose if she pushes me out, she'll be safe to keep on with her dirty little secret.

I might go to HR, but I'm fairly sure that she's best mates with Mary in that department, so anything I say to her will get back.

Charlie was OK most of the day. However, this evening after I'd cooked Alison and I dinner, I'd no sooner picked him up and smiled at him than he started screaming and didn't stop until he passed out an hour and a half later.

I think it must be me; for the last three days the same thing has happened. Charlie has been OK until I get home or hold him, then within five minutes he's screaming. The 'Colrel' drops came today and we've tried them; they've not worked straight away, but the bottle does say it can take up to twenty-four hours to work.

Sunday October 28th 2012

Sunday fear ruined most of my day today. All I could think of was work tomorrow and what could happen. It's distracting, I should be enjoying my time with Charlie at the weekends, but when I was out walking with him in the park, all I could think about was work.

I'm glad Charlie's too young to remember the face he was looking up into as he dropped off. The frown Alison told me I'd been wearing all day can't be nice for a baby to see.

I keep promising myself that I won't take Jane's stuff on, but I do time and time again. Maybe I'm mad. Alison says that she can just switch off her head from thinking negatively. Mine seems to go into overdrive at the mere mention of anything negative. I should really look into that, maybe I'll get a book out about it. I'm pained to do that, though, as it's Jane that should change her ways, not me.

Monday October 29th 2012

They're definitely still at it. I saw Boris coming out of the manager's office today looking like the cat that had got the cream. He also looked like the cat that was doing his trousers up after getting the cream, too.

Boris probably believes all of Jane's wild stories about how much she's done in her life. It's all nonsense, though.

I thought about popping into the library on the way home from work, but Alison texted me saying she needed nappies and someone else to hold Charlie.

I haven't seen her wound up with him before, but he had been crying all day and was still crying when I got home. I don't know if it made it worse or better that when I got there and held him, he stopped. I don't suppose it made her feel very good. My ego went wild for a while, but I couldn't help but remember each and every time that it'd been the other way round. I think I got a few minutes of peace from him before he went to sleep and Alison requested I put him down.

We went into the kitchen; she wanted to talk to me. I think she just needed some support and for me to tell her it was OK to feel stressed. Tomorrow I'm going to ring my mother and ask her to come round and sit with Alison a couple of hours a day. She's not working all the time, so hopefully between her and Alison's own mum, who mine will tell – there's no doubt about that – they should be able to sort something out.

If I'd bothered to prepare myself in any way, shape or form, I could have saved a bit of money from a better job and had it ready for such events. If I'd done that, I could have got an au pair. I could have taken more time off than two measly weeks. I could have paid for some classes in how to cope. There are so many things I could have done better than I have. Alison says that I shouldn't worry about what I could have done, but concern myself with what I can do. This nearly caused a row as it felt like a bit of an attack when she said it. I told her that I was doing everything I could, that I was trying to improve our situation and that it was hard. She reminded me that it's probably harder for her than it is me, which is true, she's the one Charlie wants in the night, she's the one who gets up with him pretty much all the time, first thing, and she's the one that spends all day with him.

I'm going to try and spend as much of the weekends as possible with Charlie. I'm going to get up early and try him with a bottle so Alison doesn't have to. I've spent most of my life and most of the pregnancy looking forward to the weekend so I can have a lie in, and Alison has allowed me to do that even though she's been awake with restless legs or feeding Charlie.

Alison was right, I need to look at what I can do now, and one of the things I can do is try and get up early so Alison can get some more sleep. Maybe I'll even see if I can work out a system whereby Alison gives him his teatime feed then goes to bed, and I give him his bedtime one. That way she should be able to get more than an hour's sleep at a time and I'll feel like I'm actually doing something to help, other than putting up with dickheads at work in order to get money. Much more fatherly, I think.

Now all I've got to do is take the action. Talking about it to a piece of paper is all very well, but there needs to be some action.

Tuesday October 30th 2012

When I'm walking up and down the hallway with Charlie in the night, I've got a lot of time to think about stuff. I've started to wonder if Boris is as stupid as he seems. I mean, if I was an alcoholic who needed regular lie downs at work and still needed to actually get paid, then I suppose one way of making sure that happened would be to get in with, or more literally 'in' the boss. He's played a blinder, the more I think about it. Not only does he get an easy ride, he also gets free alcohol in the form of cooking wine. It's perfect for him. I actually think he's probably been manipulated by Jane in some way or other. I know he will think he's the one doing the manipulating, but the more I see of Jane, the more I think she's a bad person to the core.

NOVEMBER 2012

Saturday November 3rd 2012

As promised, I got up when I heard Charlie screaming this morning. Thankfully, he stopped when I picked him up. Alison had just about woken up. It was pleasing to be able to tell her to go back to sleep. Me and Charlie spent all of ten minutes in the lounge watching tele before he started crying for his breakfast. It wasn't the 'in pain' crying, which was good, but I really wanted to let Alison have a lie in and I couldn't as he wouldn't take his bottle from me. He just doesn't want to eat anything from me. Alison has two options, breast or bottle, for him to choose from, I only have one and he isn't interested in it.

Charlie didn't cry this evening until he wanted feeding. I think we might have solved the colic problem.

Sunday 4th November 2012

3.00 a.m.

The potion was a fallacy. Charlie started screaming again in the night and didn't stop regardless of what we tried. It's an absolute nightmare. I'm starting to wonder what we were thinking about, thinking that we could bring up a child; two completely inexperienced people with barely an ounce of sense between them. We're probably damaging Charlie beyond belief with all our bumbling about and inability to help him when he's in pain. I bet people who are in stable relationships are much better parents. I bet they spend years planning out how they're going to do things and working out rotas and such like. Us? We had no time to do any of that. We didn't have time to even get to know each other properly before Charlie was here.

I bet other parents don't have it as bad as us. I know that it's not easy, but surely Charlie is the most upset baby in the world and it's all our own fault.

8.00 p.m.

I got up early with Charlie again this morning and this time took a bottle with us while we went for a walk. Putting the winter clothes on a baby while trying to allow his mother to have a lie in is a task in itself. Charlie doesn't seem to like getting dressed. I went for quickness over trying to placate him while I went along. He seems to cry anyway. Then, once he was in the pram and out the door, I headed straight for the bumpy path that led to the park. To my amazement once we were on there he stopped screaming and started looking up at the trees. He was fascinated by the swaying branches. There was a little smug look on his face, then when I called out his name, his focus came to me and I could see there was a little smile at the corner of his mouth. I'm sure that's what it was, anyway. We walked for an hour in the park and for nearly all of that time, Charlie was asleep. It's the only thing he can do when he's in the pram.

There was a downside to all the sleep in the park, though; it meant as soon as the motion of the pram stopped when we got home a couple of hours later, Charlie was wide awake. Alison was just getting up and it's amazing what a couple of extra hours of unbroken sleep had done for her. She looked great and once she'd fed him, she went for a shower while I made silly noises at the baby, trying to get the smile back on his face. I didn't manage it this morning, but once I told Alison that I'd definitely seen a little smile from him, she made it her mission to get another from him, and later on, she did.

Maybe the walk in the park first thing was good for Charlie. All the bumps certainly seemed good for his body, as when I was holding him later he did a double-loud poo which almost came out over the top of his babygro. When I cleaned him up, the poo had gone everywhere, up his back, all over and inside his gentleman's bits and pieces, and in the folds of his little chubby legs. He also managed to get his feet in the dirty nappy when I was changing him. In the end it became clear it was a two man job and I had to call down to Alison for help. We doused him down with the shower attachment in the end, it was the only way to be sure we'd got it all. The little smug look was there again as we were cleaning him. We can safely say that we've got a baby who's able to smile.

Sadly, though, he's a baby who's able to smile, but who isn't very happy.

I've made an appointment for Charlie at the doctor again in the morning. Jane won't like it, but that's going to have to be her problem to deal with. I'm not buying into her games. Surely it's illegal to stop a new parent taking their baby to the doctor when he isn't well?

I need to check out the personnel policy. Jane's told me to read it before, but I've no idea where we keep it. It's not like there is a PC in the kitchen for chef to check his email. There's a folder somewhere with all the policies in. I'm sure it'll be fine. I feel I've got enough power over Jane now I know about her and Boris's dirty little affair.

Monday November 5th 2012

We saw the doctor and he again told us that it's colic and that Charlie'll grow out of it. I asked if there was anything at all he could suggest, but the best the doctor could come up with was wearing ear plugs.

It's the first time I've heard Alison swear (apart from at the birth).

I didn't bother going back to work and decided to spend the afternoon with my son before he started his uncontrollable screaming. Jane wasn't there, so I left a message with chef to say I was ill.

Alison has been telling me that it is more to do with the time rather than seeing me that makes him upset. She's right, too, this afternoon I held onto Charlie while we listened to the radio, and I even managed to give him a bottle of Alison's milk that she'd got ready for us. Alison spent the afternoon in bed. It was nice to be able to do something to help. I spent most of the time trying to make Charlie smile. Just after tea I woke Alison up to tell her that I'd seen him smile; she told me that it was wind and that she's seen it before. I wouldn't have it and held him up for her to see, but all I got for my efforts was a load of sick down my arm. She was right.

Charlie started screaming when I gave him to Alison. It sounds horrible, but I was pleased he was screaming at the sight of someone else's face tonight.

Some inconsiderate swine were letting fireworks off this evening. It scared the hell out of little Charlie when I jumped and the bottle I was feeding him at the time got squeezed and emptied into his mouth quicker than expected.

Tuesday November 6th 2012

Jane was in a right tizz when I got in today, moaning about yesterday. She told me if I was to take anymore leave to look after 'that f***ing brat' she'd let me go.

I've bitten the bullet and filled out the complaint form; I handed it to HR as I left for the day. I've told them I can't work for her after a comment like that. Mary agreed I could stay at home until the issue was dealt with. No doubt she was straight down to tell Jane about it all. I don't care, though, I can find another shitty job if it comes to it. I suppose that's the one plus of having crap jobs.

No change in Charlie, either, although as I was home early I got some time with him before he had an outburst. He's not far off smiling properly, I'm sure I saw him move the corners of his mouth AND he didn't burp or fart for ages afterwards, either.

I didn't tell Alison what happened. I thought she'd worry, so I lied and told her that the grill had broken so we had to close the kitchen.

Wednesday November 7th 2012

As Alison thought the kitchen was still closed I didn't have to lie to her much today. We spent the day cooking a meal and watching a film, although we had to keep pausing both to deal with Charlie. We were halfway through *Iron Man* when Charlie did a power fart, then another, and then I felt the warmness creeping out his nappy and up his back. He seemed pleased to have got it out. I hope he's not like Boris. He laughs and smiles when he's been for a poo, too. Normally he'll come out the bathroom and tell us all about it, size and everything.

The dinner we cooked turned out alright, although we didn't time it too well. By the time we were ready to sit down and eat, Charlie was in pain again. I held him and tried to comfort him. I held him like a rugby ball, with my hand under his belly, and walked about. It seemed to work for a little while and he went from screaming to sobbing. I read on the Internet this morning that if you time the crying it may not last for as long as it feels. It's a good piece of advice as he was only screaming for the twenty minutes Alison took to chew every mouthful of her dinner six hundred times and then for the five minutes it took me to eat mine at normal pace.

The poor little chap cried himself to sleep again within the hour. As he was dropping off he was still sniffling. I couldn't help but start blaming the NHS. I don't know what to hate them for, but it's got to be their fault somewhere along the line. The burning hatred stayed with me until the early hours. I was sure them pulling Charlie out like they did must have had some impact. My concerns were verified by Google after I couldn't sleep and got up.

I bet Alien warlords don't have to worry about telling their partner they're a failure. I bet it's a case of just telling them how things are going to be and letting them deal with it. I'm sure 21st century Britain has taken things too far in civilisation. I'm not being sexist here as I'm sure women have the same worries about telling men when they've lost their jobs, too. There's just too much nicety. Too many people worrying about what other people think of them. I've still not decided what I'm going to do tomorrow. Maybe I'll just get prehistoric and tell Alison the truth.

Thursday November 8th 2012

We tried another potion that didn't work, it's been another complete failure. We tried and we failed. My kitchen cupboard (that I normally keep crisps in) is now full of treatments for colic from around the world. If you're from the future reading this, you may well have solved this problem in your own race and if you have I applaud you. We haven't been able to in the few thousand years we've been around so far. Maybe the dinosaurs knew what plant to force feed their young, but we've never worked it out. I suppose it's because babies can't talk and you can't very well go round opening them up and looking. Well, if you're a warlord from the future you probably could, but I'm not sure you'd be doing it for the same reason as, say, a doctor.

There is still one more thing to try, though. I spent the remaining two hours of the evening searching the Internet, yet again, for more ideas on how to cure colic. There is one thing I've seen a few times, which seems to be dismissed by all but a few diehards, but they swear by it. That is, osteopath: the use of. Now, I thought you went to see one of these when you'd put your back out lifting something heavy. Like Boris did when he tried to carry three drums of fat up the stairs on his own to show how strong people called Boris are. But it turns out that when a baby is born and pulled out with forceps, that actually damages their little heads and the skulls don't sit properly as they are forming into a normal head shape. This made sense when I read it. Back when Charlie was still in the hospital, they said he might not be feeding properly because he had a headache; what they meant was, they'd given him a headache by yanking him out with huge metal tools clamped around his head.

I read more and more into it and it seems that, although a little expensive, the treatment does work for some people for whom all else fails.

I've found a place and at £90 a time it's fairly expensive, but to be honest, if we can stop the pain for our son, it'll be worth it. Not to mention stopping the screaming.

I rang the clinic and they'll see Charlie on 13th November. I told Alison and she agreed it was something worth sticking on the credit card.

I think this is the only option left to us.

Friday November 9th 2012

I'm a bad person.

I was trying to comfort Charlie tonight while Alison had a shower and he started screaming and wouldn't stop. I tried all the different ways of holding him that I've seen Alison use, but nothing worked. I ended up holding him under his arms in front of me and tried to get his attention by saying his name, this caused him to move up a gear, which in turn I did. Before I knew what was happening I was holding my baby in front of me while shouting his name. Both of us were worked up to the point of explosion. I knew I had to put him down and get out of the situation. I put him on the bed and left the room. I thought he had been screaming in the highest gear he could have been, but it turns out there is another one which I think is called 'distress'. It only took me two seconds to feel awful about myself and I went back into the room and picked Charlie up, but by this point he was past inconsolable. Alison came out the shower soon after and she took him and managed to calm him down.

I'm shocked, Diary, as I never thought I would be able to harm my own son. I didn't hurt him physically, but I made the situation worse for him when I should have made it better. Alison hasn't spoken to me since and I think she is upset with me.

Charlie seems to have forgiven me. He looked me with his big brown eyes later, it made me melt. I hate myself even more. He has no idea what is happening in the times when he's screaming and there's me shouting his name thinking that it'll magically make him feel better.

I've always thought people who hurt their babies by shaking them or throwing them on the bed were deranged, but to be honest I can see how it happens. I'm glad I was able to put him down when I did. The people that are in prison for harming their baby must feel even worse than I do now. Maybe there is a group that I should go to, to learn how to be more focused on making my son feel better rather than just wanting the noise to stop. Am I just learning? Is this the way everyone feels?

I don't think I can talk to anybody about it. I'll be arrested.

10.00 p.m.

I've been Googling. There is something called shaken baby syndrome. That's when people harm their babies. There's loads online about it and most places suggest doing exactly what I did if things get too much. It still doesn't feel right. Nature must need changing or something, parents should have something inbuilt that stops them being able to harm their young. Alison seems to have the patience of a saint. Maybe it's just me that hasn't. Maybe I'm a psychopath. I hope not.

Saturday November 10th 2012

12.30 a.m.

I've done an online test and I'm not a psychopath. I've also joined a forum and posted a post about tonight's events. Hopefully someone will answer and let me know that it's normal to feel the way I did.

2.30 a.m.

There have been five answers, all really supportive and all non-judgmental. Two were from fathers who were in the same position and did similar things. I feel better now and will get some sleep.

Monday November 12th 2012

A letter from work.

'Dear Mr Peterson,

Following on from the incident at work on Tuesday 6th November where you refused a direct instruction from Jane Bishop. You were then seen leaving the premises without her consent. I am writing to confirm your suspension from work. You are invited to a disciplinary hearing on Friday 16th November to discuss your position within the company.

You may bring someone with you to the meeting, be it a colleague or a union representative.

May I remind you that you are not to speak to anyone from the company apart from Jane and myself.

I look forward to bringing this matter to a close.

Yours faithfully,

Mary Swindler

HR'

That bitch Jane has screwed me over. In fact, she and HR have. It was Mary that said I could go home.

If I lose this job I'll have no money, then I'll become an even worse father than I already am.

I haven't shown the letter to Alison yet. I'm going to, she can't go on thinking that I'm on leave. I don't like lying to her but I don't want her to think I'm a failure.

I spent the day looking for jobs. There were some in the local homeless hostel; I haven't applied though as it said experience was needed. I'm not sure if talking to Jerry is classed as 'experience'.

Tuesday 13th November 2012

Alison took Charlie to his appointment today, I actually sat in the library reading a book on counselling and how to listen to people. I'm planning on being really good if I manage to get a job through the agency. The book spoke about being honest, but not so honest that it would hurt people. I couldn't get this out of my head and spent the afternoon walking in the park thinking about how I could tell Alison that I no longer work in the kitchen. I didn't come up with a solution.

Alison said Charlie screamed while she massaged his head and torso. However, this evening I was sitting with him and he didn't scream until later on and even then I think it was because he was hungry.

Alison caught me looking at the job description for the hostel worker tonight, and she said I should apply. I told her I haven't got the experience, but she said I was making excuses.

Wednesday November 14th 2012

Alison has forced me to sign on at an agency. We went there today, and apparently they are the guys that supply the hostel with temps when they need it. They have taken me on! We needed to lie a little bit about my experience and Alison explained that I was also good with children. They supply young people's hostels and children's homes, too.

I've got to go back in tomorrow with my passport and a list of all my old addresses as they are going to police check me to make sure I'm not a paedophile or anything unsavoury like that.

I still haven't told Alison about work. I'm scared she'll think less of me. I have the meeting on Friday.

Thursday November 15th 2012

I left home at the normal time and told Alison I'd be popping into the agency at lunch time. I spent the morning in the park. I couldn't think of anywhere else to go, it was only when I walked past the library on the way down to the agency that I realised I could have been sitting in the warm, for free, and been entertained with a book.

Giving my details to Kelly at the agency didn't take long and before I knew it I was out on the street again. I gave Keith a bell and we ended up going for a pint. That turned into three, then six and I went home smelling like Keith had chucked a pint over me, which he had.

Alison was out walking when I got home and I decided that the best thing to do was sleep it off. I woke up an hour later and she was asleep on the sofa with Charlie in her arms.

I got away with it.

Friday November 16th 2012

I headed to the appointment at work, arriving well before I needed to be there. I think I knew things were going to be bad when security wouldn't let me in the building, but made me wait outside until the time I was due, when Mary from HR came down and took me straight into the nearest meeting room to the door. It was also the furthest meeting room from the kitchen, so I didn't get to see anyone.

I argued my case against Jane, but she just came back with lies and talked about the unexpected absences and how much time I'd had off. It was interesting to see how much she changed in the situation, fighting her corner in a very manipulative way. She told the room that she'd offered nothing but support to me and the rest of the team, that she'd always been a manager that people could come to with their problems (there were nods all round) and that she was baffled by the way I had behaved as she didn't understand why I hated the job so much I would make it a misery for those around me.

I asked why she thought it was appropriate for her to shout at us and to treat Boris differently to everyone else. She denied this was the case and accused me of being jealous of a hard worker's 'can do attitude', even citing how he'd hurt his back. The whole hearing was a farce from start to finish and made me want to get up and leave. I couldn't, though, I kept telling myself that I needed this job and needed the money. I would never have been able to sit through it without knowing I needed to feed Charlie.

Then the inevitable happened; they told me I was no longer employed by them, that I would be escorted from the building, and I wasn't to return. Jane would collect my stuff from the kitchen area.

This was when I thought it was time to pull out the ace card. I put it all out there, all the times I'd seen Boris with Jane heading into an office or the store room, I put out a few dates and pointed to the CCTV camera outside the room. Jane's face was a peach. She was wearing the universal features of someone who has been caught out. I can't deny that it felt good. In that moment, looking into her face, I almost forgot that I'd just been sacked.

Mary asked to see Jane outside. They returned a few minutes later, Jane with a totally new expression on her face. It was like when I'd first met her, there was no air of superiority, no looking down her nose, she just sat there not giving too much eye contact.

Mary explained that in the light of the allegation I'd made, they would need to investigate; however, it seemed clear to her that things between Jane and myself were irreparable and that it would still be best if I wasn't there. She put her offer on the table.

My contract would run for three months, after which it would be terminated, but I would get the three months' pay as a lump sum. On top of that I would get all holiday owed to me as a cash payment. It would be explained to HR as an advance. I wouldn't be expected to be at work during those three months and I wasn't to contact anyone from the company.

Sensing the ball was firmly in my court, I asked for six months' pay. They refused. I asked for five, also refused. We settled on four months' full pay, in advance. And I walked out with a cheque for almost five thousand pounds and a bag of my stuff that Jane had under her chair with her all the time.

Things are starting to look up. I could buy a new car. If I find another job even better, I'll be five grand up. You can get nice cars for five grand in this day and age.

When I got home, I decided to bite the bullet and tell Alison what had happened at work. I couldn't see the point in hiding it and, providing that I get another job, we're going to be OK moneywise for the next couple of months at least. Of course she wanted more details. To stop her working herself up into a complete frenzy and not being able to explain myself through her questions, I just showed her the cheque.

She wasn't as pleased as I thought she'd be, though. In fact, she became more and more demanding and ordered me to chase the agency and tell them that I needed work right away.

I've promised to do it first thing on Monday.

Monday November 19th 2012

We went to the park today. It's been nice the last couple of days as Charlie has times of being calm and not just screaming. The sessions with the osteopath have really done some good.

We had a takeaway this evening. I was worried a bit during the day that Alison was in a mood with me, so I decided to ask her over a Chinese.

She said that that apart from not telling her about the situation, she is happy about me not being in the kitchen any more. The only thing she is concerned about is me getting something else sorted and that the something else isn't another shitty job, but one that I can grow into.

This afternoon I rang the agency to let them know I was available for work as soon as possible. Kelly informed me that I needed to wait until my police clearance came back. I asked how long this could take and she told me that depending on how much there was on it, how many times I'd moved and how many were in the queue, it could take up to three months, but could be as soon as two weeks. She said she would let me know as soon as she had it back and assured me that there was work available. She did offer to put me onto her colleague who could find me some work that wouldn't involve a check, but I decided to hold out. I just can't get myself into another rubbish job. I don't think Alison would be happy if I started grooving myself into another rut of this particular type.

Tuesday November 20th 2012

Charlie went for a walk with my parents today and they commented on how calm he seemed. It was right, too, he didn't scream at all. He cried a couple of times when he was hungry and when he wanted changing, both of which I did while Alison got an early night.

It was bliss.

Wednesday November 21st 2012

I got a call from Kelly at the agency today. She told me that there was a position coming up at the local youth hostel. She's arranged an interview for me tomorrow.

I'm surprised and scared at the same time. This is mad, I didn't think I'd be hearing anything about work until at least after Christmas. Alison says I'll be fine and not to worry, but Kelly at the agency even said that it might be tough going as the man from the hostel is a bit of an ogre.

The interview is at eleven; that gives me time to make sure Alison and Charlie are fed and watered before I leave.

I'm going to spend tonight making sure my suit is ironed and ready and going through some of the notes I've made over the last few months from my various research sessions in the library.

11.30 p.m.

I can't sleep, Charlie and Alison are doing much better than I am in that area. I keep getting up to make sure my shirt and suit haven't creased. The truth is, everything is ready; my shoes are polished, my tie is ready tied, my suit is clean and I've got my special comb in the bathroom. There's nothing worrying about it will do. That doesn't stop me doing it, though. I think it's some kind of illness. Alison doesn't worry like I do. Just writing this has now set off a new worry; I am now worried that Charlie will turn out like me and be one of the world's worriers, too. I'm going to stop thinking about it, which means I also need to stop writing about it.

I just hope that I can pull this out the bag tomorrow.

Thursday November 22nd 2012

I didn't sleep very much at all last night. It was a blessing when Charlie woke up just so I had someone to look at. An actual person that wasn't an evil figment of my imagination. I couldn't feed him or stop the need for Alison being up, but it was better than lying in my sweaty bed thinking about what on earth I was going to say in the interview.

I was ready to leave the house at nine, which was a bit of a problem as I didn't actually need to leave for another hour and a half and I couldn't hold Charlie or do anything else that might involve getting my suit dirty. So I just sat in the lounge waiting for the time to leave the house to come round.

Alison found my eagerness most amusing and kept on waving her jam on toast at me, going 'ooooooooh' like she was going to spill it.

I was glad to get out the house. I had to wait a couple of hours, though, as I figured that there'd be less danger in the house than in the town. Although I couldn't walk as it was raining and that meant more time sitting in the car just concentrating on how many ways there were to mess this up. I finally made it to the hostel at about twenty to eleven.

As I sat waiting for the interview to start I was what can only be described as 'accosted' by someone called Zoe who'd recently moved in after getting booted out of one of the other hostels in town. She was more than keen to tell me about the scars on her arms and how she'd got them. She was so open about it I started to wonder if she was drunk. I was smiling politely, nodding along, but being careful not to nod so much that she'd think I was endorsing her negative behaviour. I asked her what it was like living there, she said it was OK and that the lads there pinned less porn to the notice boards than they did in the last place she was in. Before she could go any further, a man in the woolliest cardigan I've ever seen was shown out by an older woman, who wished him luck before turning to me and asking if I was Graham. Zoe told her I was before I could get a word in and I was taken through to the office.

The interview wasn't the normal type I was used to; normally I turn up and talk to the chef or gaffer, they ask if I am reliable and a couple of other questions, then they offer the job. This was different. There were two people sitting behind a desk, an oldish woman and a mid-forties guy. They were each holding a pad with questions written down on it.

They were tough questions; for the life of me I can't remember more than the first one now, I think my brain has blocked out the whole experience. I didn't like it at all and felt like I was floundering all the way through.

At the end they asked me about Zoe and what she'd been talking about. I had a bit of conflict inside; I thought I might get her in trouble if I told them and I didn't really want to do that, but in the end I decided if I was going to start lying now, then God knows where I'd be in a year if I got the job, so I shared what she'd said. Craig, the guy, asked how I would deal with that if she said it to me while I was on shift on my own. I answered the way I thought anyone would, I'd talk to her about whether she'd done it recently, I'd check she wasn't in pain, physically or emotionally, and I'd try and find someone who knew how to deal with that sort of thing. I knew I'd done well when they both smiled at me as I finished saying what I was saying. Their smiles almost made me get on my soap box and start waffling on some more, but there was a fainter voice inside that advised calm. I'm glad I listened to it, as I'd run out of sensible things to say.

It was handshakes all round as I left, in the knowledge that if I'd got the job I'd hear by the end of the day.

I hadn't even got home when my phone rang. It was Kelly from the agency to ask how I'd got on. I told her it went OK, I thought, but was hard work. It was then she told me that the hard work had paid off and that I'd been offered the job, and that they were happy to wait until my police check had come through before I started. It was a temp to perm position, which means as long as I don't mess it up in thirteen weeks they'll take me onto their staff. It's more money than I've ever earned before, too, just over ten quid an hour.

Alison was over the moon when I told her and ordered that we celebrate with a takeaway.

I wasn't going to argue with that. I was over the moon too.

Friday November 23rd 2012

I was helping Alison to change Charlie this evening and as soon as we took his nappy off he started to wee; it was like a fire hose had been switched on, it went all over him, over his head and onto me. (I was standing at the head end as I thought I'd be safe from getting anything smeared or spilt on me.)

I've learned a couple of lessons tonight: 1) Always be primed and ready to cover him up again with the nappy you've just undone. If he's going to wee, he'll do it early on. 2) Don't look out the window when you're supposed to be helping change a baby, you can see the nasties coming then.

Charlie wasn't bothered in the slightest. I had to wipe his face quickly as he was grinning soon after the initial shock of getting warm liquid in his face. He does love bath time, though.

Saturday November 24th 2012

People keep turning up offering to do things for us. Dad was round earlier just to check if we'd thought about what sort of shed we wanted building. I can't even remember him offering to build a shed, but I soon realised why he was round; he'd come for a sneaky hold of Charlie.

Charlie was peaceful for a bit and seemed to enjoy dribbling on someone different for a while. He soon started screaming, though, and me and Dad realised that it was time to go into the garden and talk about sheds while Alison popped a milk bag out and fed the little mite. I've decided I do want a shed. Carpeted, with a chair. Just somewhere to keep for myself. I've realised why Dad has his shed now. It's for some peace and quiet.

This afternoon Alison's mum just popped in on her way to the shop. I've got wise to this, though, and had the big shop list ready. She flinched at the sheer enormity of it when I handed it over, but as there was a baby being handed with it, her displeasure didn't last too long. I took Charlie back off her after a few minutes, claiming that I needed to change him. I didn't, though, I just wanted some of the Red Bull that I'd written on the list when she knocked on the door. Everyone needs a bit of motivation though, don't they?

She was gone a good hour and a half. When she came back she was carrying more bags than I've ever seen a single person carry. Her fingers could barely hold Charlie by the time she'd finished the three trips to the car and back it took to carry all the shopping in. I'd have helped, but I didn't have my shoes on, so I couldn't.

She didn't stay long after, as she was being selfish and moaning about needing to put hand cream on, so I didn't get to have the bath I'd planned.

Monday November 26th 2012

I rang Kelly from the agency today to see where the police check was at. I'm keen to start. She said she was rushing about today, but would check and let me know by the end of play tomorrow.

Tuesday November 27th 2012

Kelly called this afternoon, she said that the guys that run the checks for her hadn't heard anything. I asked if I was likely to see it this side of Christmas. She said it wouldn't be unheard of for it to take that long, but she was hopeful that it would be before. She reminded me that Craig was happy to wait until the check was back and told me to take it easy.

I should try and take her advice, really.

Wednesday November 28th 2012

I had a panic today: what if work interferes with college? I called Kelly and asked her what she thought. She told me that as the course was only twelve weeks, I would still be working for her, so she could cover any shifts that clashed.

It seems like it's all coming together.

DECEMBER 2012

Saturday December 1st 2012

Alison asked me tonight what I want for Christmas. I've not really thought about it. There's nothing I really want. A good night's sleep would be nice. There's nothing material that I think I need. She suggested a new bag for college. It's not a bad idea, I've asked for one that makes me look like a mature student. I asked her what she wanted and she replied that I should know that.

I don't, though. I did think for a while that she wanted an engagement ring, but it's all a bit *too* soon. I think it would be better to have some time before we get married. She's never even hinted at that, though. If I've read the situation wrong, she might say 'no' if I ask. That would just be awkward for everyone.

Sunday December 2nd 2012

Alien warlord, I have no idea. How can I just know what she

wants for a gift? I bet in your time you've given up on futile holidays like Christmas. I should think you've also given up on all kinds of religion. I suppose, since you know that you're not the only ones in the universe, it's all a bit pointless. Us humans have had literally thousands of gods over the centuries. They all have one thing in common; they are claimed to be the one and true God. I strongly suspect that most religious fanatics are mentally ill, especially the ones that claim God has come and spoken to them. I'm not talking your day to day people, but the ones who start religions based on meetings with 'God' that funnily enough no one else was around to see. I'd like to think that in this day and age, we as a race are growing out of it. And don't get me wrong, I don't disbelieve in there being some kind of higher power in this world, I just don't buy into any of the human made religions. They cause too many problems. Not like war or anything, we'd find another reason to fight if it wasn't in the name of one or other of the gods, no, I mean like Christmas. I've GOT to find something that Alison wants or else, and it's all down to religion if you think about it enough, which I have been.

Although I will say, Warlord, if you're looking for something other than violence to control your people, then making up a religion seems to have worked pretty well so far for us.

Monday December 10th 2012

I've still not had the police clearance back. The last week has been good, though, Charlie is now able to laugh on demand (providing you do something silly), so I've spent a lot of time holding him and walking about showing him things. Kids are great, Charlie is just as fascinated with the mirror every time I show him it, it's like the first time he's seen it all over again. He loves it. I'm going to enjoy this while it lasts as I'm sure it won't be long before he gets bored with a toy in minutes.

Saturday December 15th 2012

We decided ... well, Alison decided that this was the day we were going to put up all the Christmas decorations we don't have.

As you've probably guessed, I was tasked with going out to get a tree and picking up some decorations from Alison's parents, while she cleared a space in the lounge. I bought a fake tree, about five foot tall: not massive, but it'll suffice.

I didn't stay at Alison's parents' long, I didn't want to get into a conversation about the pros and cons of fake trees versus real ones.

Once I was home I got to work putting all the tinsel on the tree. The lights took what seemed like hours to unravel, but once I did I managed to get them wrapped around the tree. I put up a few bits of tinsel all around the living room too, and with that we were decorated.

Alison spent the evening writing out loads of Christmas cards; I turned the lights on after Charlie's bath and he was completely mesmerised. He really liked the Christmas tree and all the shiny lights, so much that I'm going out tomorrow to buy loads more, I'm going to turn it into a grotto.

Sunday December 16th 2012

As planned, I went out and bought as many shiny, light up items as I could get. The pound shop has no end of things cheap. Charlie loved the look of the living room. I turned them all on while he was in the bath with Alison so when he walked in the room it was all lit up. He was shaking with excitement. He just didn't know where to look first.

I think I might even enjoy Christmas this year.

Friday December 21st 2012

I spent most of the night walking up and down the landing with Charlie, as he was suffering from wind. I had my headphones on so I could think while we walked. I racked my brains, but for the life of me I still can't think what it is that I should know to buy Alison for Christmas. In the end I moved my thoughts on to how I can get her to tell me without upsetting her. Guesswork is out, there's no way I'm going to just buy something and hope for the best. She's unpredictable and I don't want a full Alison mood on Christmas day.

I tried to ask her to confirm that I should know what she meant in a light way, but Charlie started screaming before I could get an answer. Later, when he'd calmed down, I asked again, but Alison just spoke to Charlie about me in her baby voice. 'Daddy's a silly boy, isn't he? Yes, he is, yes, he is.' Lord knows. It's like she's playing a game with me. I'm sure we've never even discussed Christmas before. Maybe it's a trick and that there is some old tradition that new fathers have to get mothers something specific for the first Christmas.

I'm braving the shops tomorrow. I think I'll pop round and see Mum before and see if she knows of any rules. She normally knows more than me about most things so it's a good starting point and it'll stop me thinking about it tonight.

I need some sleep, I'm having Charlie again tomorrow night.

I'm quite the modern man, staying up with the baby two nights in the same week. There is a TV show out there just waiting for a forward-thinking father like me to feature on, I'm sure of it. Maybe they'd even pay me for my time.

Saturday December 22nd 2012

I popped in to see Mum and asked what the magical thing Alison expected me to get her was and was met with another question: 'What has she been going on about most since Charlie was born?' I was none the wiser.

I walked into town, I wanted time to think. I was racking my brain for what it could be. I'd almost made it into town when I decided the only thing I could do was ring Alison and just demand she tells me and stop messing about. She didn't answer. I decided to get all of Charlie's toys, the few things we'd agreed the grandparents deserved, and a little something for Keith. It was as I was standing in Boots that I saw a sign advertising massage stones and I remembered the one thing I'd been zoning out from for the last three months. Alison has been whining on about her back hurting. She'd been dropping hints as well as moaning.

As I fought my way through Mothercare – and it was a fight – there was an incident. There were packs of women out hunting. There was a moment when I was scared for my life. I picked up one little babygro that had 'I'm a cheeky monkey' written on it; it was the last one. A woman rudely snatched it out my hand. When I asked for it back she started calling me a racist at the top of her voice. All her mates gathered round me and started joining in. I'm not sure where she got that idea from, she was the same skin colour as me. It worked, though, I wasn't hanging about to be screamed at. I picked up a different suit for Charlie in another shop. It was more expensive, but there were no racial slurs thrown at me.

Town was so busy, I hated it, so I headed out – then remembered I needed to get Alison's present. So, vowing to do online shopping next year, I took a deep breath and went back into the centre. I had no idea where I'd find a massage for her. I walked the length and breadth of both floors in the centre. There was nowhere that screamed, 'We sell back massages' at me.

Eventually, I saw a little Chinese medicine shop. They were only too happy to sell me a voucher for five massages – the number they said would sort Alison's back out 'No probwlem'.

As I headed to the car park, I almost had a breakdown when I remembered I'd walked into town. The taxi rank was a ten minute walk away, but it was too far. My hands were killing from all the bags.

I've never sat in a coffee shop, restaurant or in fact a pub on my own. It's just one of the things that I judge others for so would never do myself. Today I broke that rule. There was an open air coffee shop in the centre and the seats were inviting. I headed in and set the mountain of bags down at the table and waited to be served. After five minutes I put my hand up to ask if they fancied serving me anytime soon. When the surly teenager noticed, I saw her roll her eyes before coming over to tell me that I needed to go to the counter to order and pay. This caused its own problems as I had all my presents scattered about the table. I didn't really want to leave them, but I was informed that I needed to buy a drink to sit there. The waitress flatly refused to watch my stuff and the queue was heading away from my table; queuing was not good for my anxiety. I eventually got a coffee and back to my table without being pillaged. The coffee was awful. I'm still upset that it cost almost a fiver for the cup of sludge that they gave me.

I could sense all the other blokes that were out doing their panic shopping were mentally calling me a loser as they walked past, feeling superior to the people that didn't have enough friends to take for a coffee. I didn't care as much as I always thought I would, though.

Tonight I had to try and wrap the presents quietly, which with my skills was more than I could manage. Alison had to take over. This made me feel bad, as she already does more than enough with Charlie all the time.

It should be a good Christmas, though. The grandparents have invited themselves round for the day.

Sunday December 23rd 2012

Keith came round to exchange presents today. It's the first time he's seen Charlie when he's been able to open his eyes. Keith has always claimed to be good with children. His mum had a lot of babies and there was always one crawling round the house the entire time we were growing up, so I just let him hold Charlie without dishing out any instructions. As soon as Keith had Charlie in his arms he turned into a camp version of Graham Norton. All the faces he was pulling were so funny. Charlie loved it, he was full of smiles. I took the opportunity to question Keith's sexuality while Charlie couldn't understand what we were saying. Keith turned round to tell me what he thought of me and when he turned back Charlie had positioned his mouth to where Keith's mouth landed and then he was sick. A full milky sick right from Charlie's mouth to

Keith's. I was so happy.

It turns out that isn't all that uncommon, though. Keith wasn't fazed; he just lowered his head and let the sick fall out of his mouth and onto our floor. I couldn't complain too much, though. I too busy laughing.

Tuesday December 25th 2012

Head hurts, too much Baileys. I'll update tomorrow.

Wednesday December 26th 2012

Drunk …

Thursday December 27th 2012

So Christmas day, then …

Charlie left an early present for me in his nappy, which I got to open as soon as he woke us up at half past four. I thought kids his age were not supposed to know it was Christmas or be able to get over excited about it, but it seems that is wrong as Charlie was an extremely happy baby on Christmas morning.

I left Alison to lie in and I got Charlie up and fed him his first bottle of the day, which he didn't cry for. He just waited patiently on his mat, looking over to me to make sure I was doing it right. His eyes were firmly on me. It was a nice bit of bonding.

After I'd fed him and burped him, and wiped the sick off my chest, I put him on the play mat and tried to get him to roll over. He's now able to grab hold of my finger and uses it to pull himself around. His little legs go in the air and he just pulls as hard as he can, while lying flat on his back. This means that he rolls on his side. He wasn't quite laughing, but it was almost there. He was looking at the faces of some trees on a toy Alison has laid on its side near his mat. He likes them.

Once I'd seen him almost laughing, I thought it would be a good idea to see if I could get the full belly laugh out of him. I know he smiles when I run my finger along his top lip, so I put my finger near both his lips and moved it up and down while making the 'bupah, bupah, bupah' noise. He was smiling so much. Then the smile turned into a frown and then a cry. I think I tickled him and he didn't like it. Either that or he literally laughed so much he scared himself.

The early morning turned into normal morning and Charlie glued his eyes to the cartoons on the television. The cartoons are extremely boring and, in fact, patronising for a baby of Charlie's mental calibre. I switched off in the end and slipped a *Simpsons* DVD on while Charlie was asleep. He wouldn't notice the difference and while I can get away with not watching *Mr Happy's Christmas* – I will.

Alison woke up about eight and made us some egg and ham rolls. It's a Christmas tradition in her house to do that so I had no problem forgoing the Christmas tradition I had of having no breakfast at all and being insanely hungry all day until dinner. Alison shocked me during breakfast. She opened the Baileys she'd been saving until she stopped breastfeeding completely. I had a glass, too, but made the mistake of necking it like a shot. I started doing the cough you do before you hurl up whatever it was that made you cough in the first place and Charlie woke up with a jump. Once he saw it was only me having a bad time of it, the biggest smile in the world spread over his face. If it wasn't for the fact he did a huge belch as soon as Alison picked him up, I might have thought he had a wicked sense of humour.

We decided to wait until our parents arrived to open the presents. Sue had decided she was doing all the cooking, with the help of my dad. Looking over at the size of the pile of Charlie's presents made me feel a bit jealous. If it wasn't for the fact I knew they were all cheap baby toys, I'd have been really upset. Especially when I could see the two gifts for me, one of which was definitely a book on how not to lose control. Keith buys me some sort of self-help book every year for a joke. He finds it funny to suggest I'm stressed, on edge, or – as was the case last year – pulling my own hair out. Later I found out this year's was called *How Not To Fu~*k Your Kid Up*.

The parents turned up about 10.30. I could hear the tittering through the window well before the door knocked and Bill jumped through the door wearing a Father Christmas outfit and shouting 'Ho, ho, ho'. It didn't last too long as our hall is really narrow and he started stepping all over the shoes we keep near the door. If he hadn't had me to hold onto, he would have gone over. My own father was carrying the biggest dead bird I've ever seen in my life. Bill had bought it, but had given it to my father to carry as he didn't want to ruin Charlie's first image of Father Christmas. I knew the second I looked at it that it wouldn't fit in our oven. I didn't say anything, though, I didn't want to ruin the moment. He was obviously proud of having found such a beast.

They'd arrived together and when we got talking it turned out they'd all spent Christmas Eve together in the pub and then gone onto midnight mass. The cooking commenced once Bill had made Charlie cry by shouting 'Ho, ho, ho' in his face. Alison ordered him to remove his outfit after that.

Later I heard Bill shouting from the kitchen that we were going to have to do a bit of surgery to get the bird to fit the oven. When he then shouted through to ask if I had a saw, I went in to discover a bit of a blood bath at the kitchen table. He'd not found the sharp knives and, instead of asking, had gone to work with his Swiss army knife, which wasn't enough for the job in hand. I handed him the biggest knife I had, the one that comes in every knife set that seemingly has no other use than chopping a gigantic turkey in half.

Once we'd managed to do that, Bill started to bag up all the little bits of turkey that hadn't managed to survive the battle. He said he'd be using them for a curry tomorrow. I vowed to myself there and then to never eat any curry made by him.

The grandparents were cooing over Charlie and fighting for the right to hold him and try and make him laugh. Then, when it got too much for him, they argued through the means of baby talk over who would hold him. 'You want this granny to hold you, don't you, don't you,' I heard Sue telling my mum, as Charlie cried.

I suggested that he might need a nap and took him upstairs. I didn't tell them I was going to have a little nap, too, but I did.

I came down about 12.30. Charlie didn't need as much sleep as I did and it felt worse than if I hadn't bothered. Still, the industrial vat of Red Bull that I necked helped a little bit.

The present stack seemed to have grown while I'd been upstairs. It seemed the grandparents had brought a truck load with them to go with the masses they'd given us beforehand.

We decided that, as the huge half a turkey was barely warm, we'd crack straight on with the presents. Alison and her dad had been at the Baileys while I'd been asleep, I could tell by the way she was dancing to a Christmas album from the 80s.

The present opening took over two hours. I don't know how the grandparents managed to keep the fake excitement painted on their faces for Charlie to also get excited over. They did, though. I started on the Baileys at around present number forty-seven, having decided that since we had some babysitters for the day it'd be a good time to get stuck in.

Alison's parents didn't see the humour in Keith's gift to me and weren't backwards in coming forwards about it either. 'I just don't think it's very funny,' Bill said rubbing his bald spot. I tried to explain that it was just banter, but I was drowned out by the next present for Charlie being unwrapped.

All in the all the present opening *was* great. Charlie was so excited to see all the toys and books he got. He loves faces and there were a lot to look at and smile at. He even talks in his gobbledygook to some of them. It's great to see happen.

I gave Alison the gift I'd spent ages agonising over, but she didn't seem too impressed. I thought it was a good gift. I didn't get the chance to point this out, though, as she had to go to the bathroom; she must have eaten her breakfast too fast.

There was very little crying from anyone during the afternoon and once the turkey had been hacked up even smaller, at about four, it finally started cooking and we ended up sitting down to eat just after Charlie had been put down for the night.

Sitting around the table with our parents it made me feel ever so grown up. There we were, all parents, and all linked together by that one bond. It would have been nice if Charlie had been there, but as he can't eat food I don't think he sees the point of a table, except when he's sitting on it. The conversation turned to what we'd like Charlie to be when he grows up, I'm fairly sure that whenever we sit down from now on, this will be a feature. It's not the right time for me to think about what I want for him when he's older, though, as I just want him to be a happy baby now instead of one that screams all the time. Both sets of parents have high hopes for him: doctor, lawyer, district judge, all job titles that are highly above what Alison or I are educated to. I hope the schools are good, if that is the sort of hope that's being pinned on him, as he won't be learning about law or medicine at home. I know Alison's a nurse, but she knows about old people, not medicine.

The meal turned into the inevitable game of Christmas Monopoly. Charlie screamed on and off most of the evening, which meant one of the grandparents was away from the table most of the time. I used the opportunity to slip notes from the bank when no one was looking, but I still lost the game in the end. It must have been a combination of karma and really poor dice throwing skills. Everything I made from my crimes just went to the other players with houses, as that's the squares I kept landing on. Maybe it was my cavalier attitude towards purchasing that did me wrong, although I blame that on the Baileys.

I woke up on the sofa Boxing Day morning to hear a loud banging on the front door. Looking around I could see Bill on the floor, but no sign of anyone else. Charlie started screaming as I was making my way to the door, so I knew there were more people in the house and it wasn't just me and Bill, which pleased me as for a minute I was worried I'd spent the night exclusively with him.

I answered the door and it was my neighbours. They wanted to know if I was going to make a habit of having wild parties and men getting changed in my garden. Apparently their visitors had been most upset to pull up outside on Christmas morning to see the sight of a near naked Bill struggling to get into a Father Christmas outfit. I think it was the hangover that did my thinking as I just wished them a happy Boxing Day and closed the door. I hadn't had a clue what they were on about at the time; I was still wondering if I was awake or if I was dreaming. The amount of Baileys I'd had the previous night was nothing like what Bill had put away, though. The kitchen looked like there'd been a student party in it the night before. Cans and bottles were everywhere.

Alison told me later that I'd been singing *We Wish You a Merry Christmas* at the top of by voice long after everyone had gone to bed, or home in the case of my parents and her mum, Sue. Charlie had slept through it all. Alison said that her dad had given him some Baileys. I was angry about this, but she said that he'd slept right through without waking her up, so once we'd shut up she was able to get her first full night's sleep without being woken up every other hour since Charlie had been born.

Today was looking like a write off after I relapsed into hangover mode around lunchtime, but Bill introduced me to the hair of the dog, telling me 'What makes you bad, makes you better'. He was right, too. Well, the first shot came back up in the kitchen sink, but the second one stayed where it should and I started to feel better; by the third I was singing again. I had to stop, though, as it was upsetting Charlie and his screaming was upsetting me.

We spent the day in the working men's club near Alison's parents' house. There was a cold cuts buffet, which seemed to have been provided by the customers. Everyone had just brought all their uneaten meat in with them. The disco was pumping and as Charlie wasn't screaming we stayed for a bit. The drink was flowing. I haven't been on a bender like that in years. Bill poured a large Baileys into my pint, and that's the last thing I remember until I woke up at home this morning.

Alison told me I was just absolutely wasted all day. More than once she had to stop me taking Charlie onto the dance floor in his pram. All the patrons knew Alison of old and wanted to hold Charlie. He loved the attention, apparently, which is strange, as he normally hates a lot of noise. I suspect that Alison or Bill slipped a bit of Baileys in his milk. This has been confirmed by Alison demanding we buy a new bottle of Baileys today.

I need to Google the effects of giving a baby alcohol. I can't just take the word of Bill and several of his heavy drinking friends in the working men's club. Charlie has been quiet, though.

Friday December 28th 2012

10.00 a.m.

I've checked online. It says it's not a good thing to give babies alcohol and that the rumour that it helps them sleep is an old wives' tale and shouldn't be listened to. I'd have to dispute that; I've seen it work. I can't understand it, I was reading it on the BBC website and they're run by the people … they wouldn't lie to us, would they? I'm confused now.

13.00 p.m.

I've spent the last three hours checking other sites and even found myself registering on Mumsnet.com. Everyone there agrees with me; it does help babies sleep. Well, it knocks them out, if you want to get technical about it. It also does their insides damage. I found a post that explained in language I understand. It said:

'If you can't give your baby food for four months, as its stomach isn't ready for it yet, what do you think the chances are of it being ready for burning chemicals?'

The BBC site is widely discredited on there for wrongful information. I might email them and let them know that they've got it wrong. They wouldn't be giving out that sort of advice if they knew, surely. I might even ask for a day or two's discount on the licence fee. I'm sure they'll thank me for pointing it out.

Alison didn't take the news well that I was removing the Baileys from the bedroom. She was almost pleading to be allowed to still administer it. I didn't realise she was so desperate for sleep. Luckily I was armed with the facts and was able to tell her about Calpol. The mums on the Internet swear by this for the nights when they really need sleep, but they don't just dose the babies up all the time. Alison's argument was that when she was a baby, she'd been given alcohol to help her sleep and that there was nothing wrong with her. It stumped me a bit as I hadn't realised that her parents' attitude towards alcohol and babies wasn't a new idea; they'd been knocking her out with the stuff when she was little. We didn't row, but we agreed to disagree on it. I left the room then realised that probably meant that she would be still giving him Baileys, so I rang my mum for advice.

She said if Alison is thinking the only way she can get a night's sleep is by drugging the baby, then maybe I need to do more as a father and have Charlie in the night more often, with bottles.

She's right, and I'm having him tonight. Alison took the bottle of Baileys into our bedroom and left me to it. I suppose old habits die hard.

8.00 p.m.

Charlie is sleeping at the moment, so I should get to sleep. I'm a bit excited about doing it, to be honest.

10.00 p.m.

Charlie woke up at 9.15. He stayed awake screaming and refusing to have his bottle until fifteen minutes ago, when he stopped screaming, necked his bottle in one, and passed out again. I didn't sleep before then, I just kept checking his breathing. Alison will kill me if she wakes up to a blue baby in the morning.

Saturday December 29th 2012

12.00 a.m.

I've just fed Charlie again. He didn't cry for as long this time. I'm going to try and get some sleep now.

01.30 a.m.

Charlie is in with me, now, he wouldn't sleep on his own. I'm still awake and he's due a feed in half an hour.

02.10 a.m.

I still can't sleep; I'm terrified I'll squash Charlie. I've got on the floor now and left him asleep in bed, surrounded by all my pillows and all the cushions from the sofa. I can't say I'm comfortable. Maybe a Baileys will help me drop off.

06.30 a.m.

Charlie slept for three straight hours in bed, then wanted feeding. I couldn't get him to drop off again after his bottle. He was up and ready to get on with his day. He'll make a good postman when he's older.

Alison got up at six and sent me to bed. The floor wasn't very comfortable and I can't have had more than an hour's sleep all night.

It's not as easy as Alison makes it look.

04.00 p.m.

I don't know how Alison does it. I've been in bed nearly all day and I'm still shattered. I could hear her singing to Charlie downstairs when I woke up. It sounded so beautiful. It reminded me of my own mother singing to me. I've been getting little feelings and flashbacks recently. Like tiny thoughts of things that I remember from being little. The singing is one example. When Charlie was trying to get to sleep and getting frustrated with it, I got the feeling that I knew what that felt like. I can't say that I remember totally trying to force myself to get to sleep, but there was something there, just a brief memory of really trying and getting angry that I couldn't force sleep upon myself. It's strange. I don't know if I'm mystic or not. Up until recently I thought my earliest memory was falling over the kitchen step and hitting my knee. I remember it as I was allowed to choose the cakes for tea. We had Mr Kipling blackberry and apple pies, I think. Anyway, it seems the tasty treat memory has been replaced with struggling to sleep. I hope it has, anyway, or I could be going mad.

10.00 p.m.

Charlie knows he has us wrapped around his little finger. Tonight we were putting him to bed. Same routine, but he has had a bit of diarrhea so we were worried that the screaming was wind or something. Alison picked him up and the first thing he did was stop screaming. He hugged his mother and nuzzled into her shoulder. When she was walking away from me I looked into his eyes, he caught my gaze and he knew I knew he was playing. A little grin formed in the corner of his mouth. Then as quick as it came it was gone again. The little swine. It was a good trick though. I'm proud of him.

Monday December 31st 2012

1.00 p.m.

So, it's the end of the first year me and Alison have been together. We didn't have plans to go out this evening so I've spent some time reflecting on things. When I think back to how I was a year ago, not just with my work situation or relationship status, but where I was mentally, I didn't even think about other people at all. I thought about myself. Sure, I was aware of other people, but in the last twelve months I've had a woman come into my life, then shortly after that a little baby boy. Within twelve months I've gone from being a singleton who was rubbish at talking to women, to being in a serious relationship, and a father. It's mental.

I've been thinking about how fast time goes. I've found myself saying a few things lately that up until I said them I thought 'older' people said. I saw one of Keith's little brothers and was holding Charlie at the time. I said, 'I remember holding you when you were this age.' The look on Keith's now teenage brother's face was the same look I used to give when family friends said it to me. The way things are going I'll be rolling out all the grown up clichés before long. I suppose it's just the way things go. If I think back really hard, I can hear people saying similar things to me, followed by, 'Wow, I feel really old saying that.'

Recently I've also been thinking more about when I was a kid, I've been seeing both my parents much more lately than I did before Charlie came along, and all the stories of when I was a baby have been told. It's really shown me how quick time goes. In a mere thirty years, a new generation is born and we just relive everything that was done prior, albeit with changes to the advice given by the Government on what side to sleep the baby on, when to give them food and such like. Time really does compress as you get older; when I was younger the thought of having to wait a week for something was dreadful, being given an extra ten minutes to play outside was the best thing in the world and the summer holidays were the Holy Grail of holidays. Now they fly past before I know where I am. One day I hear that the kids are off and the next thing I know they're back and it's safe to go into town again without bumping into the 'indie' kids outside Subway. The more I think about how quickly time goes, the older I feel.

Dad says that time only goes faster as you get older. I think a lot about time and how much there is of it, especially when it's compared to how long humans get to live for. It's unfair. I mean, when you think about it, time goes back to when we were monkeys; that's millions of years, and on average, as humans, we get about seventy years to play about with. It's not much, is it? It's a tiny fraction of what time there is, or has been. I've just thought, maybe you're not an alien warlord at all. Maybe you're what we evolve into. I hope not, as I doubt we humans are going to be able to invent machines that bring people back to life from the hair samples I've left behind.

I'm getting morbid now. All I can really hope for is that 2013 is as good as it looks like it's going to be. College is there, the job is there and I've got Charlie and Alison, what else do I need?

I might need to quit smoking. I'll put that on my New Year's resolution list for tomorrow. Tonight, though, I'll smoke, and I'll do so while watching my tax money literally go up in smoke over the millennium wheel on BBC at midnight.

3.00 p.m.

Mum texted me asking me if I was going to ask Alison to marry me tonight. I replied asking her why she had even thought about it, and she said that Alison's parents had told them that it was the one thing she was hoping for at Christmas and that she was disappointed when I didn't get her a ring. Shit. I didn't think it was the right time, what with the baby and all the other stuff we've been dealing with. It's something I've put to the back of my mind. Sure, I love her, but I haven't even got a ring to give her, even if I did want to.

I replied asking my mother if she'd have Charlie for the evening.

5.00 p.m.

I've got nowhere to take Alison, The grandparents are all having a boozy night in at my parents, my mum has agreed not to get too drunk and is having Charlie. I've just got back from dropping him off. Alison is still asleep. I've managed to get my great grandmother's engagement ring and I'm set to go. This must be the weirdest relationship going. All the grandparents know the proposal is going to happen before the intended fiancée. The only good thing about that is that Bill gave me his credit card and told me not to worry about how much anything costs. I was going to ask him if that extended to an Internet shopping excursion, but decided it wasn't the time for jokes.

6.00 p.m.

I've managed to book a table at the nicest Chinese restaurant in town, they still had loads of tables and didn't seem concerned about it being New Year. I asked if we'd need to be out for a certain time and they confirmed we could stay as long as we wanted. Alison is awake now and is getting ready. When I told her the plan and that we'd been given the night off looking after Charlie, she looked sceptical. I've got until eight to get ready and practise bending down on one knee. I rang Keith to let him know what I'm going to do. His cheering and whooping almost caused me to hang up the phone; even though I was locked away in the safety of the bathroom and he was on the other end of the phone, it was so loud I was sure Alison could hear it. After I'd finished shushing him, he asked if I'd thought out a strategy. I informed him that I had got as far as deciding I was going to do it and booking the table, that was it.

'Well, you'll need to plan when you're going to do it. Are you doing it before the meal, during, after? If it's after, you need to make sure it isn't raining as if it's wet you'll look like a fool standing back up again in those white chinos you insist on wearing on special occasions.'

I didn't know people noticed I only had one pair of going out trousers. I'm almost thirty, I'm not in my teens with a different outfit for every time I'm out.

'Is there anything else I need to know?' I asked Keith in a hushed voice.

'Loads, if you've only done that. Have you practised kneeling down in the trousers yet? Have you ...' And so it went on for fifteen full minutes of advice on how Keith thought things should go. Seriously, the bloke should be a wedding planner or something the way he went on about it, the excitement he had, not for me or Alison, but for the event. I wouldn't be surprised if we got there tonight and saw Keith lurking about outside the window watching it take place.

I'd been in the bathroom so long talking to Keith and then after that practising getting down on one knee that Alison knocked on the door to see if I was OK. I'm ready to go, all I need is Alison to finish messing about with her make-up and hair and we're off.

I've got it all planned out, I'm going to ask Alison to be my wife tonight. I just hope she says 'yes'.

The End

ABOUT THE AUTHOR

Pete is 33 and lives with his wife, Lucie; daughter, Lilly; and their pet sofa, Jeff. He's been writing for just under three years and they've been pretty eventful; well, more eventful than he thought sitting on Jeff, typing, would be, anyway.

First published in the *Radgepacket* anthology with a story he'd written during month five of his new hobby, Pete's now featured in a total of ten different anthologies and has been amongst some very fine company. (Although he was the best in all of them, he knows that because both his mum and Jeff told him and they're both honest-to-God Christians … possibly.)

Author of comedy e-books *The Village Idiot Reviews*, *The Office Idiot Reviews*, *The Idiot Government Reviews* and *More Village Idiot Reviews*, Pete has seen these books sell more than he ever thought they would, and he's hooked. *Dating in the Dark* is Pete's first self-published novel. His traditionally published novel, *So Low, So High*, was published by Caffeine Nights in June 2013.

Contact Pete:

Facebook:
https://www.facebook.com/Pete.Sortwell.Author

Twitter: @petesortwell

email: petesortwell@googlemail.com

OTHER TITLES

THE DIARY OF AN EXPECTANT FATHER

Not only is Graham Peterson unlucky in his choice of careers, he's also been terrible with women throughout his adult life. That changes when he meets Alison on a work night out. Unfortunately for Graham, however, things change so drastically that within a month of dating Alison he gets the news that he's about to become a father for the first time.

The Diary of an Expectant Father charts the months leading up to what should be the happiest day of a young couple's life, but with a relationship so new and a career so bad, can Graham keep everything together for the sake of his unborn child?

With all the pitfalls and worries of an expectant father charted, this book is for all those who have been through pregnancy or just want to know how a man deals with all these things internally.

SO LOW, SO HIGH

Most people generally don't drink white cider for breakfast, don't use the aisle of Tesco as a toilet and don't steal from their family and friends. Simon Brewster does though. He's a doomed man. Living life day to day, stealing Edam balls and legs of lamb, ducking and diving his way from petty theft to dealer and back again. If he doesn't change his ways, he'll never see middle age, let alone old age.

He's seen his parents on their knees, crying, begging him to stop; he's been arrested by his former best mate; he's been hospitalised, all as a result of drugs and alcohol. It's just not enough to make him stop.

Simon lies to everyone, including himself. The truth is, he has no more idea why he does the things he does than you do. What he needs is a way out. But if such a thing exists, Simon hasn't had much luck finding it. He's powerless and his life is unmanageable to the point of insanity.

This is the story of Simon Brewster's last year using class A drugs. Join him as he crashes his way through police cells, courtrooms and display cabinets. One way or another, Simon will stop using drugs. But can the people that love him help him overcome his addictions before his addictions destroy him?

Available from Caffeine Nights Publishing.

THE VILLAGE IDIOT REVIEWS

Join Brian as he tries to woo the girl that works in the local shop; will passing out face down in super glue while trying to make her a gift hinder his chances of getting her to go out with him?

Will Father Frederick, an alcoholic vicar who has a slight issue with stalking, be able to win back the heart of a woman he loved a long time ago?

And will Ethel, who thinks that throwing hard rice instead of confetti in a bridegroom's face is an acceptable form of sport, be able to catch one of these two losers in love with her trick as they step out of the church on the happy day?

Written entirely in the form of product reviews, we guarantee you've never read a book quite like this before. Hilarious and wholly original, *The Village Idiot Reviews* pokes gentle fun at the more obscure corners of your favourite e-commerce sites – and introduces the most bonkers set of countryside dwellers since The Vicar of Dibley.

THE OFFICE IDIOT REVIEWS

There are all sorts of idiots we have to work with every day. Every office has them. Fortunately for most of us idiots in the work place are few and far between. However, Hogsbottom Plugs, 'the home of bath plugs' has a higher concentration than other workplaces, from the MD down to the cleaner, they're all Idiots.

Read the trials and tribulations of this idiotic workforce as they explain their recent life events through reviews of things they've bought. There's Donald, who try as hard as he does, simply cannot get the office junior to notice him, let alone drink some of his special, sleeping tablet-laced tea. Learn how Jeff gets his own back on the people who mock him by re-enacting a video he saw on YouTube involving seagulls, and watch in horror as the over-worked cleaner tries to solve the mystery of who is making his job of cleaning the toilets worse than a job cleaning toilets is already.

If you've ever worked in an office, then this is the book for you. You'll recognise the office sex pest, the liar and the moaning admin worker who's been there longer than the chairs. Written in the form of product reviews, *The Office Idiot Reviews* is the second in the series of 'Idiot Review' books from Pete Sortwell.

THE IDIOT GOVERNMENT REVIEWS

We've all seen the news over the last few years, watching in wonder and disbelief at the situations the people entrusted to run the country get themselves into and then proceed to lie their way out of. Just imagine, and this won't be hard, that they were so stupid that they wrote reviews of the items that got them into or out of their latest bit of trouble and posted them online.

Ted Williebond is angry, not only at having to settle for running the opposition, but also for the bullying he had to endure at school by Cameron Davies and Gary Osburn, who now run the Government and don't mind pointing that out to Ted every time they see him. Join Ted as he foolishly leaves reviews of such items as Silly String, vodka and thick curtains as he tries his hardest to bring down the coalition.

On the other side of the fence we've got Daniel Dangly, a foolhardy old school politician from Southamptonshire who, try as he might, cannot outrun the press, who seem to stalk him for easy stories; and Elouise Munch, a career girl more concerned about who's defaced her designer handbag than the people in her constituency.

Running the show though isn't Cameron Davies or Ted Williebond; in fact it is Betty Rivers, the CEO of Information Inc.

THE COMPLETE IDIOT REVIEWS

The first three 'Idiot' reviews books are now available from Amazon in e-book format as a handy box set.

MORE VILLAGE IDIOT REVIEWS

It's been a year since their last outing. Brian, Ethel and Father Frederick are back with more village idiocy.

Frederick has injured his nipples in a vicious moped accident whilst on his honeymoon and no longer feels like a man. He's taken up the drink again and is making people's lives a misery with his antics again. He can't work out why strange men keep following him while he's out drink-driving, though.

Brian's concentrating on getting through married life while trying to find a hobby that doesn't hurt. His cousin Jeff (from *The Office Idiot Reviews*) has moved in for the summer and is on hand to help Brian with his assertiveness when he is bullied by the local biker, Jock.

Ethel has discovered that it was Denny who made her shopping trolley explode last year and with Denny now an adult and living outside the safety of the children's home, it won't be long before she exacts the revenge she's been after.

Meanwhile a battle for power is taking place at the manor house. Lord Monty, who ordered his title from the Internet, is in a battle of wills with his gamekeeper, Chopper. It's a never ending struggle which, time after time, leaves Monty either out of pocket, in pain or soaking wet.

Written entirely in the form of product reviews, we guarantee you've never read a book quite like this before. (Unless you read the first one.) Hilarious and wholly original, *More Village Idiot Reviews* introduces the most bonkers set of countryside dwellers you've ever had the pleasure of meeting.

DATING IN THE DARK: SOMETIMES LOVE JUST PRETENDS TO BE BLIND

Jason is single and has been for all of his 32 years. It's depressing. But not as depressing as being told by his mother that he looks like Humpty Dumpty – after the accident. With a face that not even his own mother can love, it's hardly surprising that he'll try anything to get a woman to go out with him, even if it's only for a single date.

With little interest in anything other than his quest for a woman and a nice bit of cod and chips, Jason needs to think outside the box if he's going to find someone who'll give him a chance. Along with Barry – his best mate – Jason comes up with the only thing he thinks will work: dating a blind woman.

However, to do that, he needs to pretend he's blind himself, which is a lot harder than you might think ... especially when guide dogs are so hard to come by. Eventually Jason's efforts pay off and he meets Emma, a pretty professional with a host of friends. When he takes her out, they instantly hit it off. But will Jason be able to fool both Emma and her best friend Jerry into thinking he's blind? With everything to play for, Jason faces the biggest challenge of his life, and nobody – especially not him – can see how it'll all turn out.

BRIDE AND GLOOM: SOMETIMES LOVE IS BETTER OFF BLIND

In the first book of the 'Sometimes love …' series, 'Dating in the Dark: sometimes love just pretends to be blind', Jason Harding thought he'd committed the ultimate betrayal. No, not cheating; he pretended to be, you guessed it, blind. For Emma, the woman he was stupid enough to think he was fooling, it wasn't anything like a betrayal. It was both sweet and sad at the same time and, as people in relationships have a tendency to do (if they don't split up because of one party's wild lies), Emma and Jason decide to get married.

Just how Jason manages to deal with the huge life change that is marriage is what this book is about. From getting his specially made suit tailored to his short height, to trying to keep a lid on his best man's plans for a wild weekend in Liverpool, he is going to struggle to make to through to the wedding without having a full nervous breakdown. His second best friend, Boris, also returns in this book, although he has lost his taxi, his wife and his ability to seem sober even when he's drunk six litres of vodka.

Jason is foolish enough to add Neil, Emma's wayward cousin, and Terry, the owner of Jason's favourite fish and chip shop, to his list of groomsmen. This is the fairly tragic band of men that are to ensure Jason makes it to the church on time, in possession of both his of his eyebrows and, of course, the rings …

Printed in Great Britain
by Amazon.co.uk, Ltd.,
Marston Gate.